"Bill gives it to you strai
able information from h

Herb Thompson, c   *g ... best-selling author,*
Green Beret, and U.S. Army Drill Sergeant of the Year

"Leaving the military, especially after over 20 years of service, is a daunting journey. This book is a helpful resource that reminds us to see our journey from potential employers' perspectives. Use this advice to inform your transition from the military to an exciting and fulfilling new path."

Tony Cerella, Ed.D., Lieutenant Colonel, U.S. Army

"This book should be standard issue when active-duty military members are one year from leaving service. Its insights are clear and relevant, providing guidance to help solve any career transition issues."

Michael Halterman, Marine Raider veteran

"Bill channels his inner Sun Tzu, describing the 'chaos' of transition, but also the 'opportunity.' Take the opportunity to read Bill's insights. Learn a great deal about the process of transitioning. Bill's book should be on the tables of every Military Transition Center, used by corporate HR teams, and shared with executives."

Dr. Steven Horsley, DEL, Assistant Professor,
University of Charleston; Former Commandant,
Joint Special Operations University Enlisted Academy,
U.S. Army Special Forces (Retired)

"Finding the right fit for me and my family after military service is the most difficult thing I've ever done—more difficult than MIT; more difficult than selection into the pararescue community; more difficult than a 20,000 ft. nighttime HALO jump. I learned many of the lessons in this book the hard way. Regardless of whether you have a few years or a few hours before you take off the uniform — pick it up, read, and heed. You'll be glad you did."

Ryan Castonia, Two Bear Capital;
former U.S. Air Force Combat Rescue Officer

"Every service member has concerns about transitioning from military service to the civilian world. I personally experienced this, and I have advised many friends, colleagues, and students about the challenges of this transition. In military parlance, Bill Kieffer provides valuable TTP — Tactics, Techniques, and Procedures — based on his personal experiences with the transition process, and his deep understanding of the employer's perspective. This guide will clearly assist readers in their preparation and execution of transition from military service and will vastly improve their understanding of the civilian employment environment. I wish this handbook had been available when I retired from active duty. I highly recommend it to those contemplating this significant life step."

Jim Shufelt, Colonel (Retired), U.S. Army; Professor Emeritus,
U.S. Army War College; Former Course Director, Nominative
Leader Course, Army Strategic Education Program

"Making career transitions can be daunting. If you are a military member, veteran, or anyone else seeking to take your career in a different direction, this book needs to be on your bookshelf. Bill provides real-world advice and practical steps to making successful career moves."

Carrie Schochet, Founder and CEO, Purple Squirrel Advisors

"This book provides a unique and important perspective on career transition. Its 'view from across the desk' has nuances that veterans must understand and master to land successfully. For example, the focus on 'language' is important and often under-studied. Bill closes the military–civilian work culture gap in a truly interpersonal, specific, and scientific way that allows service members and veterans to apply, and ultimately land with, that special organization or dream position."

Gary Steensgard, U.S. Army Veteran;
Human Resources Leader; Career Transition Mentor

"Bill Kieffer has authored a book that every transitioning veteran needs, and one that I wish I had. After 32 years of service, I felt dumped into the civilian workplace. Luck found me, but this book spells out the essence of every company's hiring process and reasoning to make sense of the situation. Every Soldier, Sailor, Airman, Marine — and anyone making a transition needs to read this book — a critical insight into their future!"

Ron Haynes, U.S. Army Lieutenant Colonel (Retired);
Chief Strategy Officer, Phoenix Global Services;
Former Head of Logistics Plans and Operations, JSOC

"This book offers so many practical nuggets of truth, insight, and clarity on transitioning from the military to the civilian workforce. Having worked in this space for over 5 years, Bill is spot on in his advice and guidance. I especially loved 'If you tell us *I'll do anything,* we have nothing for you.'"

Janie Livesay, The Honor Foundation

"Transitioning out of the military after 27 years as a U.S. Navy SEAL was the hardest thing I've done. Bill Kieffer's insights and advice are akin to being handed the best intelligence package possible on what civilian employers are looking for, and how I can provide it. It works!"

Bryan Johnson, Captain and U.S. Navy SEAL (Retired)

"If one is looking for a guide written by someone who understands what transition to civilian employment can entail, then this book should be on the list. Concise and extremely thoughtful, the topics covered should prove valuable to anyone looking for practical advice on what they should be thinking about when joining the civilian world."

Derek Leo, Former U.S. Army officer; senior executive in the financial services industry

"This book is a 'must-read' of every servicemember and veteran in preparation for their career transition. It is `intelligence preparation of the career battlefield.' Bill has successfully 'been there, done that' on both sides of the career transition desk. Reading, understanding, and putting these insights into practice will make your career transition much more successful."

Bob Cursio, U.S. Army Colonel (Retired); logistics executive and former Director of Logistics, USSOCOM

MILITARY CAREER TRANSITION

Insights from the Employer Side of the Desk

William E. "Bill" Kieffer

ISBN 978-1-7373714-0-3 (print)
ISBN 978-1-7373714-1-0 (ebook)

bill@kieffer-associates.com
https://www.linkedin.com/in/williamkieffer/
419.205.7072

Printed in the United States of America

This book is dedicated to all the men and women who have served, are serving, or will serve in the military. Blessed are the peacemakers.

CONTENTS

TRANSITION 69

TALENT ACQUISITION, RECRUITING, AND INTERVIEWING 137

FOREWORD

As a child of the "Greatest Generation," I learned from an early age about the importance of the United States military and those who serve. My father was a soldier in the U.S. Army operating in the European Theater during the Second World War. He came ashore in the third assault wave on Omaha Beach Easy Red Sector on D-Day. He fought his way across Europe and into the heart of Nazi Germany and was seriously wounded at the very end of the war. V-E Day was in his words, "One of the greatest days of my life!" I share this personal account to say that I have the greatest respect and appreciation for the military men and women who serve and sacrifice for our country.

Embedded in this quick backstory are three very important life lessons that I carry with me to this day. First, I learned that useful and meaningful information can accelerate a person's success. My father had a very challenging transition from his military career into civilian life for a wide variety of reasons. There was a lack of good transition resources and counsel back in the day, and by and large he made his transition all alone. Secondly, I learned that both character and skill sets are transferable sources of competitive advantage. Despite a truly challenging and stressful post-service transition over a number of years, my dad was able to use his military training and resiliency to adapt, move forward, and establish a meaningful and successful civilian life/career. Finally, my dad instilled in me a very valuable lesson about military service that he repeated quite often as I was growing up, "If you want something done, give it to someone who has been in the military because they have the discipline, work ethic, adaptability, and toughness to get the job done!" I learned that my dad was right!

These lessons have served me well for the past four decades as a Distinguished University Professor of Leadership, researcher, author, consultant, executive coach, and resource to senior members of the U.S. military and members of the intelligence community. I have had the privilege of conducting leadership development programming for more than 8,000 members of these communities over the past decade and have helped countless military personnel make the transition to their next career. This is where Bill Kieffer and I intersect today.

I have known Bill for 30 years as a senior HR executive, talent management leader, business consultant, and executive coach. When you couple these exceptional experiences with Bill's broad and deep experience as a U.S. Army officer, he is in an excellent position to serve as a personal coach and advisor, helping servicemen and women transition from their military careers to the civilian work world. When Bill and I discussed the ideas behind *Military Career Transition: Insights from The Employer Side of The Desk,* I was immediately excited about the content, tools, and materials that he has created to help veterans successfully make the transition.

This important book not only helps veterans prepare for their career transition; its approach helps to bridge the cultural gap that exists between veterans and their civilian employers. It clearly acknowledges that employers need to be more keenly aware of veterans' skill sets and the value-added talents they can deliver. Importantly at the same time, this book is written to create clarity and focus around veterans' responsibility to be prepared for success in their post-military careers.

Think of this book as the necessary "intelligence" that the reader can use to prepare themselves to enter a new career arena that will test their skill, preparation, situational awareness, and ability to execute an effective plan of attack.

Bill has provided some exceptional advice and coaching in this book, using five highly interrelated topics that will help you make the most of the new post-service opportunities in front of you, including:

★ General Business Insights

★ Culture

★ Transition

★ Networking

★ Talent Acquisition, Recruiting, and Interviewing

So, as you prepare for your next career after the military, think about this book as a handy "career transition intelligence briefing" to equip you for this transition. Whether you plan on starting your own business, buying a franchise, working in the public sector, or working in the private sector you need to master the concepts presented in this book to succeed on the "career transition battlefield." Equipping yourself with this key information and practices will have a powerful effect on your ability to serve yourself and your family with the same level of success and honor that you have served our country.

In closing, do not underestimate your talent and your ability to succeed in the next phase of your life and remember the words of my dad when he said, "If you want something done, give it to someone who has been in the military because they have the discipline, work ethic, adaptability, and toughness to get the job done!"

I encourage you to use Bill Kieffer's book to leverage your military talents and experiences and to help your future employers get the job done!

—Clinton O. Longenecker, PhD
Distinguished University Professor of Leadership Emeritus
People and Organizational Transformer
Toledo, Ohio USA

PREFACE

Congratulations on your military service and career!

Whether one enlistment or a 30-year career, you did something very few people do. You volunteered to serve our great country. You endured rigorous training, long days, and for many, the difficulties of deployment.

The military changed you. You learned. You grew. You were a member of one of the most highly capable organizations of any type anywhere in the world. (Which admittedly, like all organizations, has and will always have room for improvement.) You saw and did things most people never see and do. You are not the same person you were before you entered military service.

The world changed too — as it always does. New challenges arose. New opportunities came to light. Some norms were reinforced. Some evolved. Some are gone forever. The world continues to adapt.

Now here you are. On the back end of your military service. Approaching the day when the uniform comes off. For some of you, this is a day you've dreaded. For others, it's the day you've longed for. For many, it is simply the next step in your life journey.

Whether you loved, hated, embraced, or endured your time in service, one thing most veterans agree on is that the military does a pretty darn good job of preparing us to do our job: Training us in particular skills; making sure we are aware of the situation and environment we are likely to fight and operate in; and building a true community around us to support us, our organization, and our mission.

' **world.** For the first time in years,
'oaration, you are now facing an
.ew world has an entirely different
 are likely not properly prepared —
 .vorld.
 of you, this transition will be a piece of cake.
 ,aration, your personal situation, your network,
 aspirations, abilities, availability, agility, and actions
 .il line up almost magically, at just the right time, in just
the right way so that the perfect opportunity lands in your
lap.

For most service members, however, career transition
is a challenging time. You are trying your best to depart the
military on great terms: closing out your duties, ensuring
proper hand off to successors, checking the boxes for the
Transition Assistance Program (TAP), making huge decisions for yourself and your family, and so much more.

Leaving any job or career is tough. Leaving a job or career to enter a new one that is substantially similar and
that exists in a substantially similar environment/work culture is tough. Leaving a job or career with no clue what lies
ahead or where you will land is even tougher. Leaving the
military and joining the civilian employment world is often
that third case. Service members often separate from service with little to no awareness of where they plan to land
or what lies ahead.

**The civilian work culture is often dramatically different
than the military.** The languages are different, the structures, organizations, expectations, norms, players — all different. While it is all different, there are many bits of your
military experience that can be highly value-adding to the

civilian, commercial work world — IF you are ready, willing, and able to learn, adapt, adjust, and take action.

Much has been written about military veteran career transition. There are many fantastic resources available to service members and veterans to help make career transition as efficient and effective as possible. Each offers its unique perspective, information, tools, and techniques.

Transition is a road march, not a sprint. It is a series of events, which often takes longer than we'd like, and sometimes works out differently than we expect. It involves myriad new tasks, topics, people, and processes, and requires diligent preparation and training to execute effectively. Huge opportunity — if you have eyes/ears open, are willing to do the work, and able to let others in to help!

What you've been doing for the last few years (or decades) is now in your rear–view mirror, an important part of your past that has shaped who you are today, your perspective on life, and your capabilities.

You are now entering an open field. One with which you likely are not so familiar. Choices, challenges, opportunities, and obstacles are nearly endless.

The world is yours do with it what you will. Fantastic stuff! And scary...

You may choose to start your own business. You may buy into a franchise. You may take a job with an existing company. There are many great stories of huge success on all these paths. All come with pros/cons, challenges, and opportunities.

Most often, veterans join an existing organization. For this reason, I focus this book here.

This book takes a unique look at military veteran career transition — a look from the employers' side of the desk.

—William E. Kieffer
July 2021

MY STORY

I've been blessed with success on both sides of this transition. After nearly 12 years as a U.S. Army officer and having been selected for promotion to Major, my family life took an unexpected turn, causing me to choose to separate, leaving a career that I loved and that was full of positive potential.

I left with no plan, few resources, and no idea about what lay ahead. I was totally unprepared for the world I was entering. It was foreign. It was scary. It was frustrating. It was exhausting. But it was also exciting, challenging, and one of the most valuable learning experiences I could ever imagine. I learned about the civilian work world. I learned about me.

Networking? No idea. Interviewing? Are you kidding? LinkedIn didn't exist when I transitioned. Neither did many of the other great online resources available today. I pounded the streets, read newspapers, made calls. I got over my introverted self to go out and meet people; to tell my story; to ask for information, connections, opportunities.

I realized that nobody cared as much about my career as I did and I got strong.

It sucked. I sucked at it. But I kept going. I got better. My network grew.

And then it happened! I landed a job — Deputy Director, Economic Development for the county I live in. I didn't know jobs like this existed. A network connection knew of the opportunity. He matched us up. I interviewed and got the job. I am forever grateful to this man, for he saw something in me that led him and the hiring manager to believe, despite my not–so–obvious relevant experience, that I was the right guy for the job.

It was a huge learning curve, technically and culturally. I'd never done local, county, or state government work before. I was not well versed in economic development theory or practice. I did not have a huge network of connections that would likely be value–adding to the agency's mission of attracting and retaining business. But I did have great experience. I was educated. I could analyze, assess, consider options, make decisions. I could think, interact with people, handle a crowd, make a coherent presentation. I was organized, hardworking, creative, and dedicated to the mission. Turns out these were the value–adds that agency needed at that time. It also turns out that I was not uniquely qualified...most veterans hold these capabilities also!

As I did this job, I learned. I learned that the way I did business in the military was drastically different than in the real world. Some carried over. Much didn't. Most work seemed to move at an astonishingly slower pace; other things seemed to pop up and get solved blindingly fast. There was drastically less operational and process clarity, priorities shifted rapidly, and the general nature of work was far less structured and much less formal. I also learned that relationships are what get deals done.

As I did this job, I continued networking. Eventually a connection of a connection knew someone who had an open training manager job with a supply chain/logistics company. I connected, applied, interviewed, and landed a job that led to swift/steady promotions and a great 22-year career in enterprise–level HR and talent management leadership in large, complex, global companies. In this career I focused on the entire spectrum of HR and talent management. From strategic talent and workforce planning to recruiting, selection, onboarding, performance management, training and development, compensation, benefits, employee engagement, and myriad related other topics, I've been there, done that.

Today I operate an independent coaching and advisory firm focused on optimizing military veteran hiring and employment. I work with both individual veterans and employers to help each better understand the other, so that great potential and great opportunities align.

I offer this book to share insights from a guy who's been there, done that on both sides of the transition experience, with special focus "from the employer side of the desk."

ACKNOWLEDGMENTS

Writing this book has been a labor of love, fulfilling a life-long goal.

It has been fun, challenging, frustrating, and fulfilling.

It never would have happened without the love and support of my wife, Nikki, who has encouraged me, stood by me through struggle and success, and given me the encouragement and honest feedback I needed to keep moving forward.

I am also greatly indebted to all my kids — Nate, Traci, Ben, Ryan, and Jeremy — who each in their own way, whether they realized it or not, gave me inspiration to bring this book to life.

I'm eternally grateful to my parents, Ed and Mary, who taught me discipline, tough love, manners, respect, and so much more that has helped me succeed in life.

To the countless military leaders, business leaders, fellow soldiers, coworkers and colleagues, and the service members and veterans with whom I am privileged to work, I send my sincere *thank you.* Your individual and combined contributions to my journey and this book are invaluable.

My sincere thanks also to Becky, Amy, Lori, Lise, Rachel, and the entire Weaving Influence team for their expert support in bringing my manuscript, notes, thoughts, and ideas to life.

ABOUT THE AUTHOR

Bill Kieffer
https://www.linkedin.com/in/williamkieffer

Bill has coached, advised, mentored, and worked with hundreds of service members, veterans, and others around the globe regarding career transition, leadership development, and performance improvement throughout his career.

He is President & Chief Advisor of Kieffer & Associates Limited, an advisory firm specializing in Military Veteran Career Transition, Leadership Coaching, Strategic Talent Management, and Professional Speaking and Facilitation services.

He also serves as a coach and coach advisory board member for The Honor Foundation, a non-profit group providing career-transition services to the special operations community.

Bill is a senior human resources executive with more than 22 years of professional experience in multiple large, complex, global companies. His broad-ranging work includes full spectrum human resources and talent management, and coaching/advising individual leaders and teams, from the C-suite to the shop floor.

Prior to these experiences, Bill served nearly 12 years active duty as a U.S. Army officer in a variety of command and staff positions. He is a veteran of Operation Restore Hope in Somalia, supported Operation Just Cause (the Panama invasion), operations in Central America, and Hurricane Andrew relief operations. During Bill's assignment with the U.S. Army Logistics Management College, he was selected as their "Instructor of the Year." A Distinguished Military Graduate from the University of Toledo ROTC program, Bill later went on to earn the U.S. Army Ordnance Center's Herbert W. Alden Award, as the outstanding honor graduate of the Ordnance Officer Advanced Course. He was the recipient of several awards and decorations and earned both Airborne and Air Assault qualifications.

Bill is active in his community; he was twice appointed and thrice elected to public office and serves on several veteran-related organizations.

Bill was honored to present "Investing in the Middle" at TEDx Toledo in 2017. He has worked in and traveled to 32 countries — he's set foot on every continent except Antarctica. As for his personal life, he is married with five grown kids. In his free time, Bill loves riding his Harley.

GENERAL
BUSINESS
INSIGHTS

1

We've got work to do. We need people who fit and add value to our team.

This really is the bottom line. Just as the military had a mission, so do we. Whether for-profit or not-for-profit, publicly traded or privately held, emerging or established, large or small, we need capable partners, focused on helping us succeed.

Yes, our mission is different than what you are used to, but it is our mission.

The two critical criteria when we make hiring decisions are simple:

★ Can you successfully do the work we need done?

★ Will you fit well into and add value to our team?

Everything else that comes with career transition, job search, recruitment, and selection, etc., boils down to these two points.

All the other activity that often grabs your attention and drives so much activity is little more than tools, techniques, processes, systems, and paths to this bottom line.

The journey can be daunting but keeping these two basic points in mind can add helpful clarity.

2

Job openings exist because we have unfilled business needs (not because you need a job).

At some point a business leader makes the business case that filling this need requires hiring someone.

There are many reasons that may justify this decision. Often times they include:

★ New Business

    ★ Increased work volume that exceeds current staffing levels.

    ★ New work needs to be done for which internal talent is simply not capable. Perhaps a new technology or product has gained priority and new knowledge/skills/abilities/experience are required to push it towards commercialization.

★ Replacing Departed Talent

    ★ Attrition is normal. People come and go.

    ★ Sometimes their departure enables a review of staffing needs and does not require a backfill. Often, however, positions need to be filled.

★ Building a Pipeline of Future Talent

    ★ This is a more forward-thinking proposition wherein the business strategically opens positions to get ahead of anticipated future needs.

Each of these reasons comes with varying expectations and motivations. Discern them to customize your preparation and optimize your readiness to "Answer every Ask" and present yourself as the best possible candidate.

Career Transition Shared Focus = Job Opportunity
Employer Has It...You Want It

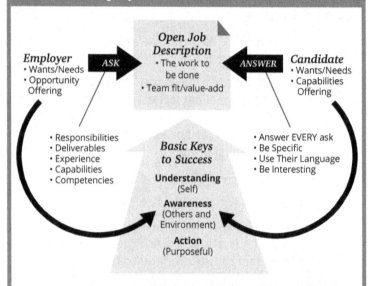

Employer
- Wants/Needs
- Opportunity Offering

ASK →

Open Job Description
- The work to be done
- Team fit/value-add

← ANSWER

Candidate
- Wants/Needs
- Capabilities Offering

- Responsibilities
- Deliverables
- Experience
- Capabilities
- Competencies

Basic Keys to Success

Understanding (Self)

Awareness (Others and Environment)

Action (Purposeful)

- Answer EVERY ask
- Be Specific
- Use Their Language
- Be Interesting

Watch-outs:
- Both parties may not know/understand things thoroughly
- Needs, wants, opportunities, capabilities may change
- Both parties may fail to communicate/articulate well

Candidates:
- Understand who you are and what you bring to the party
- Define success
- Understand transition environment
- Learn the language, transition, and hiring resources/process
- Prepare quality resume, LinkedIn profile, elevator pitch, etc.
- Network
- Informational Interviews
- Applications (online or other)
- Job Interviews

3

We (usually) do our homework before posting a job opening.

Once the business need is determined, some variation of the following process usually occurs:

★ HR and the hiring manager conduct a job analysis to understand and document the job's:

   ★ Deliverables, performance expectations, reporting structure, level, etc.

   ★ Required skills, experience, education, etc.

   ★ Relevant behavioral competencies necessary for success.

★ This analysis provides information we use to help answer key recruitment planning questions:

   ★ Timing for the fill — must this be filled ASAP or will we wait for the "ideal" candidate? (Usually this is ASAP, with an understanding that once an offer is made, the candidate will likely ask for two weeks before starting. Anything beyond two weeks, while possible, is highly unlikely.)

   ★ Sourcing strategy — Will this job be filled internally or externally? If externally, how, what partners/ sources, etc.?

   ★ Compensation — What is the compensation range and structure for this job? Internal (pay compared to other similar company positions) and external (pay compared to similar positions in the industry and geographic area) equity concerns? Base pay, variable/incentive pay? Benefits packages?

Note — as an expense, employers will always want to pay as little as possible while still being attractive to top talent.

Why is this important to you? Because you need to know that hiring is not a random exercise. It takes time, attention, and money, all of which are precious resources in the very busy civilian work world. Do your homework. Recognize that employers are always pressed to do more with less and that they need to know they are getting the top talent for their money.

4

We may not know exactly what we need done. Can you handle the ambiguity?

Most often we do diligent homework before we post a job.

We know what we expect re: deliverables, qualifications, experience, capabilities, etc.

Sometimes, however, we may not know. Perhaps a hiring manager is not as skilled at this work as possible. Perhaps there is little HR support to guide folks through this pre-work. Perhaps there are many varying potential solutions to the opportunity, and we want to shape the job to the top candidates' capabilities.

This lack of clarity can be frustrating for candidates, especially for military veterans. That said, I'll suggest that if you are willing and able to handle the ambiguity, to demonstrate to the employer that you are agile enough, capable enough, and willing to partner with them to create a value-adding solution, then you become a very attractive candidate to fill that open role. Who knows, you might even be able to help shape the role to best fit you!

5

Sometimes business conditions change, and we suspend the job opening. Sometimes we reopen it; sometimes it's gone forever.

Job openings arise in a fluid, ever-changing business context.

Opportunities appear unexpectedly. Obstacles pop up overnight.

While we strive for as much predictability and consistency as possible, there are times when we must suspend a job opening. Maybe we can't afford to hire now. Maybe we need some other job more critically than that one. Maybe, maybe, maybe.

As a job candidate, you'll likely never know why a job opening goes away. You may never know if it will reopen. You may never get an update on the status of your application. It's not fun, but it is what it is.

How do you mitigate your risk? NETWORK!

Get to know people inside the company. Make contact, create a connection, build a relationship. If/when things change, your chances of getting meaningful information are much greater.

6

Organizations have a life cycle. We are where we are. It impacts how we operate. Understand where we are in our life cycle and how you can add value.

At each stage of an organization's life cycle, different needs/priorities exist. These drive different cultures, norms, and expectations.

Being aware of these differences and how they align with your wants, needs, and preferences can help optimize your transition/search, and your success once you've landed.

For example, if you are interested in working for a fast-paced, emerging company that expects all team members to lend a hand across any task that may arise, you may be a better fit for an organization that is earlier in its life cycle. If, however, you prefer to work in an established organization, continuing established processes and procedures, making incremental continuous improvements, you may be a better fit for a more established company.

Typical organizational life cycle phases and key characteristics are:

★ **Launch/Start up** — High risk/reward, disruptive, passion, new idea(s), all hands, fast pace, change, few standard operating procedures (SOPs), etc.

★ **Growth/Expansion** — Proof of concept, revenue growth focus, operationalizing, some specialization, setting metrics, seizing opportunities, some SOPs, etc.

★ **Shakeout/Stability** — Formalizing, more structured, becoming specialized, gaining market share, operational improvements, talent focus, etc.

★ **Maturity** — Established products, steady customers, incremental growth, cost effectiveness, focus, efficiency, operational excellence, bureaucratic, etc.

★ **Decline** — Stagnant/Declining sales, shrinking margins, asset divestitures, rising debt, stagnant management save/sell decisions, etc.

Top talent is needed in every phase, but as you can see, each phase requires different focus, talent, and capabilities.

7

Getting hired is just the start of your time with us. There is a typical employment life cycle you should understand.

This cycle represents the typical stages people and organizations experience relative to their time spent together: Attraction — Recruitment — Onboarding — Development — Retention — Separation.

It recognizes and reflects that people and businesses evolve over time and their wants and needs evolve also. No one works for an employer forever. This means that businesses will lose team members (great and not-so-great performers) over time. But work still needs to be done, so the employers must fill the open jobs.

Similarly, business conditions change over time. No market, industry, product line, or organization remains static. The forces that impact business success constantly evolve and require new solutions to new challenges and opportunities. These never-ending changes drive the need for new employees and create new opportunities for top talent to join the company and make a positive impact.

Once a need is identified and the job opening is approved to fill, the cycle begins with "Attraction" — the employer taking actions to get the employment market's attention. This includes things like:

★ Ensuring the job description/posting/advertisement is written in a way that accurately describes the job and piques readers' interest.

★ Offering pay and benefits that are competitive for that type of job in that market.

★ Having an attractive work culture/environment, etc.

★ Posting the job in locations they believe will attract potential employees' attention. (Given that so few of the
civilian employers have military experience, it is little
surprise that many do not have the slightest idea how
to get their opportunities in front of military veterans
specifically.)

The cycle then moves to "Recruitment" — the efforts to
find and select the best person to fill the opening. On the
surface this is a relatively simple concept — attract great
people, screen and interview them, select the best, and
make an offer. In practice, however, this is often a laborious,
time-consuming process with many moving parts, evolving
variables, and fraught with lack of clarity, delays, and innumerable challenges. Many people have their hands in this
process, each with their own perspective, goals, and competing challenges.

Once recruitment is successfully completed (generally
when there is an accepted offer and a defined start date),
the "Onboarding" stage begins. This includes all the plans
and actions the employer takes to optimize your entry to
the organization, take care of required compliance-type
actions, ensure you are enrolled in various benefits and
other programs, and ensure you have access to relevant
facilities, systems, and resources, etc. This stage is critical
also in that it is when employers familiarize you with the organization, your team, your leadership chain, the mission,
your job expectations, and so many other critical areas that
will help get you up to speed, productive, and well involved.

The "Development" stage is an extended part of your
time with the company. Its focus is to help you perform well
today and to prepare you for success tomorrow. There are
myriad processes, practices, programs, and other activities

in this stage. As a general rule, most employers' focus on development is far less robust than the well-evolved development and career management our military services employ.

"Retention" is also an ongoing phase, focused on keeping employees engaged, challenged, and continuing as a value-adding member of the organization for a long time. Employers dedicate significant attention and resources to retaining good talent. After all, losing good people who are trained, qualified, and experienced in their jobs is expensive. The lost production, disruption of the status quo, and recruiting new talent are all expensive. Whether it is engagement surveys, open door/open communications, benefit packages, quality of work-life initiatives, or any of a vast number of other approaches, employers know that retaining good people is good business.

As with everything in life, your time with any organization will end. The "Separation" stage recognizes this end and the importance of handling it in a professional manner that is appropriate to the circumstance and respectful of both employer and employee needs.

8

Most employers know nothing about the military. Many don't care.

Well over 90% of the population has never served in military uniform. Today, only about 1% of the population joins the military.

Most of America has an entirely different life experience than you. It is neither better nor worse, but it is definitely different.

Beyond the simple lack of familiarity, people's level of "care" about the military, veterans, and the value veterans can bring to their business varies greatly.

People generally gravitate to that which is familiar. This simple lack of familiarity puts a hurdle in your transition right from the start. Thus, it is hardly surprising when busy people with broad responsibilities continue to conduct business according to their usual patterns. This may mean (among others):

★ Your atypical background, application, interview, candidacy, etc. may not rise to their "top-priority" list.

★ Low awareness of great veteran-hiring programs does not quickly improve.

★ Their organizations miss the opportunity to have great military veteran talent join them.

To help understand the employer situation you may be facing, I've developed the "Care/Aware Matrix."

It is a simple, four-box graphic to help you assess the situation you face so that you can make decisions that are best for you and your post-transition job/career. After all, who chooses to join or stay where little is known about them and little care is afforded them?

Understanding all this prepares you as a transitioning military veteran:

★ For rejection.

★ To address negative reception.

★ To let go of what initially seemed like a great opportunity to focus on other, better-fitting ones.

I recommend using this instrument not as a direct assessment when networking or interviewing potential employers. Rather, I suggest you keep the framework in mind, pay attention to how people interact with you, and perhaps

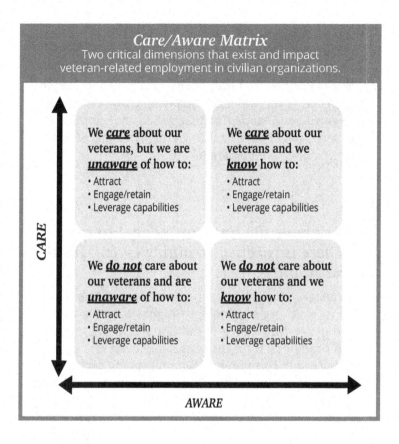

use it as a basis for broader, more general questions that may share relevant insights.

STORY

Several years ago, I had a boss who was not a veteran. He was, however, very interested in my military background and always had a positive comment around Memorial Day, Armed Forces Day, Veterans Day, etc. I appreciated his interest. One day, after the winter holiday break, my boss stopped by my office. He said, "I get it now." Having no idea what he was talking about, I asked, "What do you get?" He replied "Your military service. I binge-watched 'Band of Brothers' so I truly have a grasp of your veteran experience." I was stunned. Gathering as much composure possible, I nodded and suggested that as good as that series might have been, my experience was 50 years later and quite a bit different.

9

We don't have the time (or money) to train you. There is rarely a "training cycle." Hit the ground running.

In the military you likely became accustomed to a "train — deploy — refit" cycle. Training is highly valued and is recognized as a critical piece of individual and organizational mission readiness. It makes sense and it works!

Many civilian companies have no training cycle. We are on production all the time. Competitive pressures simply do not allow for us to disengage and train. People and teams are constantly engaged. The grind does not end.

The urgency to service customers faster, to develop and bring to market new products/services before competitors, to meet/exceed shareholder return expectations all create an urgency to "produce."

Taking time out to train is often viewed as a distraction and a take-away from progress. Certainly, the intensity level is not combat, but it is very real. For many people it is the highest level of intensity they may ever experience.

It's important to note here that in many civilian organizations, most people in positions of authority have no military leadership experience. They may have risen to their post due to superb technical skills, a highly effective network, or other valuable capabilities, but their leadership skills are not typically similar to what you experienced in the military. They may have never had a single lesson in leadership before being granted the privilege of leading people, processes, and performance.

None of this is to say that all organizations are bad or that there are no good leaders in the civilian world. There are great examples of both!

Far too often however, training is seen as a distraction from the real work that needs to be done. It is a cost rather than an investment. It may be important but many times it just isn't urgent, and we all know the dollars often go to the hottest, closest fire while longer-term, important items wait.

10

The military must "build" its talent. We are able to "buy" ours. (And when we buy, we expect you to come ready to do the work we need done.)

The military fills open positions through a well-established, rigorous recruiting process. This process has developed over generations and is continually improving to ensure mission readiness for today and tomorrow.

With few exceptions, the focus is on entry-level jobs — the front end of career paths and fields. It fills junior roles with people who are qualified for initial training and likely to succeed at entry-level roles. These folks are rigorously trained for initial success and developed over time for future growth.

General officers started as O1's (with very few exceptions). Sergeants Major (E9's) started as E1's (again with few exceptions). Each of these successful career service members experienced the most rigorous career management processes in existence to achieve their lofty positions — but they all started at the front end of their respective career paths.

Civilian talent acquisition (recruiting) works differently. While there is a general framework most organizations follow, each of them approach recruiting differently to suit their different situations and needs.

We are not restricted to filling only entry-level roles and then developing people for the future.

We get to buy talent at any level whenever the business case makes sense.

We often recruit new people to fill top jobs. Sometimes we promote internal people. In either case, we expect folks to hit the ground running, to make a positive impact fast.

Why does this matter to a veteran in career transition? I hear many veterans say they are looking for great training to get up to speed on the new job. That may happen but it isn't likely. Your new employer is paying good money to get you on the team, and they expect you to deliver. Fast.

11

You need to add value — as we measure it (technically-tactically competent).

We have work to do. We need people who can do that work, fit well, and add value to our team.

Some employers realize that veterans bring great experience, especially on the behavioral, soft-skills side of things, but if you don't understand how we define value and how we measure it, you are behind the eight ball.

Do your homework.

★ Research the jobs that interest you. Read the job postings and job descriptions.

★ Network with people who are doing the work you want to do.

★ Learn what is important, what is valued, and how employers measure that value.

★ Find out what employers are "asking" for and figure out how you will "answer" all their "asks."

12

Money drives business. You better have at least a cursory understanding.

The military does not exist to make a financial profit or to increase shareholder value. Certainly, our veterans understand the need to be watchful of spending and to make good use of available resources, but these are only part of the complex civilian work world where money is the commodity of business.

This is obvious in for-profit companies. They provide goods or services for some price that exceeds costs, thus creating profit. This deceptively simple description masks the complex and intriguing world that surrounds it. The focus on money impacts actions, decisions, and culture in ways that are foreign to many veterans.

Money also significantly impacts non-profit organizations. Fundraising, proper disbursement, compliance with non-profit rules and regulations, all are quite different than the military.

Whether your path is heading toward for-profit or non-profit, understanding the money focus and its impact on culture is important to landing in a great role and culture.

A couple of basics that some really smart folks seem to forget or not know:

★ Revenue and profit are two different things (revenue = make money; profit = keep money).

★ Taxes are expenses that reduce the profit one gleans from revenue. Like any other expense, there are numerous legal ways to reduce them.

★ Breaking the law is bad.

13

We'll always try to pay the least possible for the top-quality talent — it isn't personal, it's business. It's your job to understand what reasonable compensation and competitive benefits are.

We do a lot of work to be sure we are paying the least possible for the best return. While we generally have a pay range for open jobs to account for experience, capabilities, and a host of other variables, we're not likely to change our whole strategy for you.

Once you find interesting jobs/opportunities, do your homework to understand what a typical compensation amount and package might be for that type of job in the industry and geographic area you are interested in.

Discussing compensation/benefits is an interesting topic. Sometimes the pay range for the job is disclosed up front. Employers do this to make sure their expectations and candidate expectations are at least in the same general range. If you've done your homework, you'll know whether or not you are all close enough to keep talking.

On a related note, once you get to interviewing, don't lead with salary and benefits. Defer your responses to any of these questions as long as possible without putting progress at risk.

14

We don't speak "Mil-speak" or "Veteran-ese."

★ We won't understand it when you speak it.

★ We've got a gazillion other candidates who care enough about their future to speak our language.

★ If you don't, we're going to them.

15

We have our own jargon. Learn it. Fast.

Just like the military, our companies, industries, functions, etc., have unique jargon. Some are simple. Some are complex. It is how we communicate internally with each other and externally with our customers, vendors, partners, and various other stakeholders.

You don't have to know it all during the interview, but we expect you to have done enough homework to catch a few key phrases. We also expect you to get up to speed with it fast. Veterans have a reputation for being agile. This is one great area to prove that reputation.

16

Often there is no "higher headquarters" — you're it!

Few employers are as big as the military. Some firms are just a handful of people in one location; others may have a few dozen or hundred people scattered across a few locations; still others may have thousands of people scattered across hundreds of locations around the globe.

Often, smaller companies simply don't need a higher headquarters. People are in close proximity, working cross-functionally, and are able to handle the volume and complexities of work locally.

As companies grow, there is a push-pull between adding resources, structure, etc. and keeping costs as low as possible. Thus, the "higher headquarters" you may be used to in the military may not exist.

Where higher headquarters do exist, they often focus on strategic, outward-looking concerns (e.g., investor relations, customer relations, vendor relations, etc.) while more inward-looking, operational/functional issues are led and managed at lower levels. While this can and often does work well, it can also lead to a dearth of established guidelines, policies, SOPs, and other framework-type resources that help clarify and enable efficient, effective decision making and action.

Further, ever-present inconsistencies in business realities, organizational expectations, and discipline may render edicts from higher headquarters moot. People sometimes simply don't comply because they consider their situation unique, special, or otherwise not subject to these constraints.

EXAMPLE

The corporate strategic sales-pricing team engages in a global agreement to sell services to all global divisions of a name-brand Fortune 500 company. The pricing is level across all locations. Payment terms are set globally at "Net-30" (payment is due 30 days from invoice). Things start out great. Then a couple locations do not re-

ceive timely payment from that Fortune 500 company, thus driving up overdue receivables. Then suppliers at a few locations raise prices due to unexpected increases in their production costs, driving down margins. Suddenly, several business locations are failing to meet their P&L (profit & loss) targets. But since it is a global agreement, they can't work with their local counterparts to solve local issues. Everything must bubble up to higher headquarters. See the problem?

STORY

A few years ago I hired a fantastic U.S. Army veteran to manage our training function. He assimilated quickly and made value-adding impact right out of the gate. I assigned him a challenging project with enterprise-wide scope. Somewhere along the way while dealing with a particular topic, he asked me "What does higher headquarters think?" I replied, "Higher headquarters? We're it! What do you think?"

17

Prioritizing and planning may be very different from what you're used to. Sometimes your priority isn't the organization's priority.

By and large, the military is quite effective at prioritizing and planning. With expansive areas of responsibility that impact individuals, nations, and societies globally, and tremendous, complex internal workings, the military simply has to plan and prioritize well.

In the civilian work world, you will find the entire gamut of capability and approaches re: prioritizing and planning.

Some will use models/processes with which you are familiar. Some will have no apparent approach at all. Some will
use primary, alternate, contingency, and emergency (PACE)
plans or similarly rigorous models. Others will move ahead
almost randomly, seemingly chasing whatever whim or fad
of the day grabs the boss' attention.

STORY

*During one particularly challenging period of rapid, er-
ratic change, I met with my boss (a C-suite leader) to offer
"insight from the front" and propose solutions regarding
a significant lack of prioritization and planning, and the
impact it was having on our people and production. My
boss advised that during times of change his preferred
method was to "throw spaghetti at the wall and see what
sticks." Given my military background and natural inclination to plan/prioritize, I choked back my response.
Somehow, I maintained my composure and asked why he
preferred this approach. He replied that since things are
changing so fast anyway, there's no way to really plan or
prioritize, so we each need to just "pick a few meatballs
off the wall, work on them and hope we got one right."
When I asked him, "What happens when none of these
turn out to be the 'right things?' he replied, "Then I got
you." NO KIDDING! REAL STORY!*

 Of course, the story above is an extreme (albeit real)
example. But you need to be aware and ready for the differences in how people and organizations handle planning
and prioritizing.

★ Sometimes your priority isn't the organization's priority; e.g., you are a training manager for a for-profit manufacturing company. Your job is to optimize the capability of all employees, so they are able to help achieve business goals. Suddenly the business experiences an unexpected revenue decline. The chief financial officer (CFO) invokes tight cost control measures, including cutting the training budget (because as we noted above, this is a cost, not an investment). Suddenly your priority is counter to the business priority. What will you do?

★ What about when your priorities are different than your peers'? For example, you are a production manager focused on optimizing quality and productivity for a specific product line, for which a long-time customer is paying great margin. At the same time, Sales lands a new, high-volume, high-margin client. One that can only be serviced by your plant. Sales' priority is that new customer. What do you do?

★ You see obvious opportunities for organizational performance improvement. Your boss doesn't care. How do you react? How does this make you feel? What do you do?

Priority-related issues are notable culture-fit topics. No one is Sisyphus, the character of ancient Greek legend who was doomed to push a rock uphill for eternity. Knowing how these issues impact you and how you respond to them are important factors that help you consider and determine whether a particular work culture is right for you.

18

"Me" not "we" — the sense of team is quite different.

This is arguably one of the most frequent and challenging culture gaps between the military and civilian work worlds. Every veteran knows that we stand together. Without a team there is no success. No one gets left behind. It's all about WE.

Often the civilian world just doesn't work that way, especially in transition. Perhaps for the first time in your adult life, you are pretty much on your own to succeed or fail.

While there are instances in which some companies will espouse the virtues of teamwork, and of course individuals have to work cooperatively to keep work moving forward, the true sense of team, of brotherhood/sisterhood, of standing with your teammates in life-threatening challenges, just doesn't exist in most organizations, as it did in the military.

This difference is one of the earliest in transition to impact veterans. It often shows up on resumes. It is unfortunately very common in interviews.

STORY

Interviewer asks, "Tell me about a time when you faced a difficult challenge at work."

Candidate replies, "We were at sea about eight months. Our carrier group had been working hard. The FA-18s were flying day and night. My team of 20 people was responsible for the safe working condition of all aircrew survival equipment. The workload was very high, but we were able to work together, overcome the backlog, and ensure 100% operational readiness.

> *Interviewer responds, "That's impressive but what did YOU do?"*

You see, employers aren't hiring a team. We are hiring YOU. We have important work we need done, and we need the best possible candidate to fit in on the team and get that work done.

To be successful in transition and landing a great job/career, you need to be specific about what YOU did, what results YOU achieved. You can (and should) recognize that you were part of a team, but you must clearly point out your work and results. Rest assured, your non-veteran competition gets this point and is not making this mistake.

19

We all use job titles differently. There are some similarities but if you are focused on title, you better understand what it really means and requires.

In the military, there is far greater consistency in the use of titles. This enables consistent understanding. Veterans pretty much all know what an admiral is, what a staff sergeant is, what a gunnery sergeant is, and so on.

When you start looking at job opportunities, understand that no two job titles will mean exactly the same thing from employer to employer.

A senior vice president at a large, complex, global for-profit manufacturing company may be a huge job that requires decades of industry-specific experience. That same title in a small start-up tech firm may simply mean the incumbent is one of the top folks on a very small team working hard to make this new company a great success.

Neither is wrong, but they mean vastly different things and require vastly different experiences and capabilities.

When you are in transition, don't become enamored with titles. Look at what the jobs really are. Research the companies. Big titles may not mean what you think, and you may/not be qualified for them.

20

My job, organization, purpose, mission, and needs are just as important to me as your military career was to you.

My work and work environment may not be as exciting, as large scale, as globally impactful, or as cool as your old job in the military, but it is important to me. I spend many hours of my life at work, invest much effort, and contribute much of my talent to its success.

As you consider new job/career options, please keep this in mind: Don't discount how much I value my work. If I get the sense that you don't think it is important, I'll move on to someone else. If during our interactions you decide that my work really isn't interesting, be honest. Exit gracefully. Perhaps offer another name I could connect with. Don't waste my time. I will remember this more positively than you can imagine.

21

Onboarding/orientation isn't likely to be as rigorous as basic training.

Onboarding/orientation processes vary wildly across organizations. Some are well designed and delivered, adding value to both new hires and the employer. Many are ad hoc afterthoughts with little value add for anyone beyond the basic, "keep you out of jail" compliance stuff.

Having come from the military where onboarding/orientation are truly robust, this can be a shock for many veterans. If you experience this, carefully consider your situation. On the one hand, you may be tempted to bolt. That may be the right thing to do, or it may be a knee-jerk response that removes you from a great opportunity with an unfortunately clumsy start.

22

Work life is often mundane. Most of the time we are not saving lives. The rush of military service is rarely replicated in the real world.

There's no way to sugarcoat this. It is what it is. It is up to you to figure out how to operate successfully in this new, very different world.

STORY

When I started as training manager for a supply-chain/transportation company, I was having trouble getting excited about the job or the mission. To me we were just "kicking boxes," moving stuff from here to there. Not very sexy stuff. Over time I realized that it was more than that. We were enabling trade. We were helping businesses do business. We were helping people get what they needed to make their lives work well. Once I made the mental shift, it was much easier to be successful! I never again got the rush of military service, but I did appreciate the value we were creating and providing.

23

We owe you nothing. "Employment at will."

"Will" is the operative term. Will the employer want to hire and keep you? Will you want to accept an offer and then stay? Both you and the employer have choice. BUT options are not a given. Options arise, and one's array of options grow by dedicated effort. Employers' options to hire and fire are impacted by their efforts to be known in the employment market, their organizational culture, their employment value proposition, etc. Employees' options are impacted by their networking efforts, their capabilities, their ability to work well with others, etc.

Everyone always has choices. It's up to each of us to create options.

24

As an applicant/candidate, you need the job more than the job needs you.

We are here to achieve our business objectives...not to provide you a job.

We always need top talent, but our focus is not on you specifically. While some jobs go unfilled for extended periods, many open jobs often have dozens, hundreds, or even thousands of applicants for us to consider.

While not everyone in the recruiting cycle is a recruiting expert, it is highly likely they are far more experienced in this world than you. Keep your perspective. Do your homework. Prepare yourself.

Present yourself as the most qualified candidate to successfully do the work we need done, and to fit well and add value to our team!

25

Your career transition is more important to you than it is to us. (But if you don't do it right, we'll never know of you, and you won't be a top candidate for our jobs.)

Some of us appreciate the challenges you face when transitioning careers. That said, we are focused on our work, the future, and finding top talent to join our team. We want to know how you will help us succeed and are often not very interested in your transition efforts (beyond anything that helps us better understand how it makes you the top talent to join our team).

26

You aren't our top priority, and we don't have time to figure you out.

We have many balls in the air and many competing priorities for limited resources. Filling a particular job is often a very small bite of a very big pie.

We are running operations, keeping all the functions humming, servicing customers, attending to vendors, managing finances, dealing with investors, maintaining facilities and equipment, developing strategy, and myriad other broadly varying goals and activities.

Filling open jobs is only a part of all this. It is not a simple task. The "filling open jobs" lane alone includes workforce planning, organizational charts, job descriptions, managing suppliers and vendors, aligning internal and external players, job postings, accepting and screening applications, reviewing resumes, conducting interviews, making offers, reporting and compliance, and a thousand other things, all of which add up to the bottom line — there is work to be done, and we need people that will fit and add value to our team.

Going the extra mile to help a job applicant is rarely on the radar. There simply are too many open jobs, too many applicants, too many burning platforms, and too little time.

EXAMPLE

Let's put this in military context: Think about it — you're deployed and operating. An unknown stranger comes up and says, "I want to work here." Really? Are you going to stop operations to entertain their interest? I didn't think so.

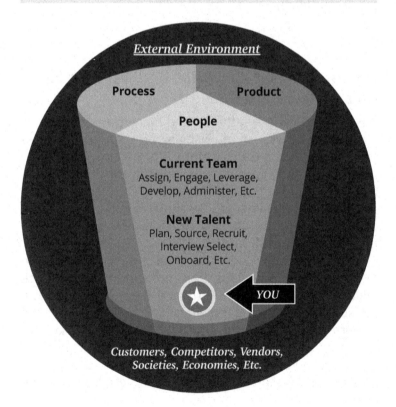

So, what to do?

- ★ Learn as much as you can, as early as you can about transition, job search, yourself, your goals, etc.

- ★ Leverage every resource possible to get known and become aware of opportunities.

- ★ Connect the dots for non-veterans you encounter along the way.

- ★ Remember, you don't know what you don't know. The employers' world keeps moving and other factors may influence hiring decisions.

- ★ Make yourself stand out. Be the candidate that understands the big picture. Demonstrate your ability to be part of the employers' solutions, not just another small datapoint on a very large, busy radar screen.

- ★ Stay positive.

- ★ Keep moving forward.

Most frequently, more open jobs are being filled by external candidates rather than internal successors. While on the surface this is a positive for transitioning veterans, the story behind the story may be concerning on two fronts:

- ★ First, this typically shifts hiring priority from entry level toward more senior jobs. (Which brings higher expectations for more exact experience.)

- ★ Second, hiring from the outside means the company doesn't have to spend on developing internal talent (scary for military veterans who expect robust career management, training, and development).

Many companies outsource the recruiting function (hiring another company to do this work), which may reduce the checks and balances on hiring managers. Thus, expectations for job requirements may become inflated to the point that mere mortals could never meet them.

Employee referrals are often the most popular method for finding talent, in some cases accounting for nearly half of all new hires. Said another way — NETWORKING is how people land jobs!

27

To be crystal clear, it is your responsibility to make it easy for employers to notice you, convince us that you are the best candidate to fill our opening, that you can do the work we need done, and that you are a great fit for our team.

Whether networking, talking to recruiters, conducting an interview, or other, you must remember "It's about them!" (Them being the other party, the employer, the recruiter, the network connection. It is not about you!)

★ What do they need?

★ How do they define success?

★ How are you going to solve their problems, leverage their opportunities, and achieve success — as they define it.

Your experience, expertise, capabilities, and competencies must make sense to them. That only happens if you focus on their needs and present your stuff in the context of their needs!

Don't make them work for it. Connect the dots for them!

What do you want to do?
What qualifies you to do it?

*Why might you be interesting
to an employer for that?*

28

Our work matters to us. Don't call our baby ugly.

Don't underestimate how important our work is to us. No, it is not the military but it is our life's work, our source of income, our purpose, etc.

We may not be as large as the military. We may not have the long, robust history the military has. But we take it every bit as seriously as you took your military career (or perhaps even more so in some cases).

When you engage with us, don't try to demonstrate how smart you are by leading with a critical analysis of everything you'd "blow up" on Day 1. Yes, we are looking for people to help us improve, but we are NOT looking for smart-ass critics who lead with harsh, minimally informed dictates.

Listen to what we say. Ask where our pain points are. Ask what our priorities are. Ask how we need you to best help us.

Just don't call our baby ugly if you want to be part of the family.

29

Biases are bad but they exist; help us overcome them by your actions.

Biases are perceptions or prejudices in favor of or against one thing, person, or group compared with another, usually in a way considered to be unfair.

Biases come from innumerable sources and are often very hard to overcome. They impact every segment of life in ways great and small. They are very real in the transition environment.

It's often said that perception is reality. In this case it is true. The vast majority of people you may deal with have never served in uniform. They know what they know, good or bad. They may have gotten their information from television shows or movies. They may be very confident in their base of knowledge and very committed to their perspective ("I have an opinion and I'm quite fond of it").

Common Biases:

* ★ Concerns that veterans have post-traumatic stress disorder (PTSD), traumatic brain injury (TBI), mental/emotional concerns that may negatively impact work.

* ★ Perception that veterans are less likely than average to obtain education, and thus may not be suitably qualified or capable to perform effectively.

* ★ Military veterans are too rigid, not flexible, and only follow orders.

* ★ All veterans are "combat vets"; combat veterans are "damaged goods" and thus present a risk in the work environment.

★ Military experience does not relate to civilian job needs (in some cases, true, but many skills do translate directly, and others are well aligned with the skills employers most want).

Of course, as veterans, we know that many of these perceptions and biases are not accurate. Nonetheless, they exist and have a real impact on whether or not you become aware of opportunities, get interviewed, or get hired.

So, how do we know where the bias exists and its extent? Of course, no one advertises their biases. It is up to you to have your eyes and ears open to the possibility and extent of their existence at your target opportunities. I'm not talking about cynicism. That doesn't help. I'm talking about awareness, the simple realization that biases exist and may become an obstacle. With this awareness you can then decide whether an opportunity is right for you and if so, how you might assess and counter any biases.

30

Applying online is generally a waste of time. You want to work here? NETWORK!

STORY

Veteran candidate says, "I know what I know. I know what my resume means."

Employer with open job says, "I know what I know. I know what my job posting means."

Neither knows what the other knows or what the other means.

Neither has the time nor inclination to figure out what the other knows.

So:

★ Great veteran candidates get overlooked.

★ Non-veterans (who are familiar with this dance) get noticed.

★ Great jobs go unfilled and the cycle continues.

UNLESS each takes action to understand the other and communicate in a language the other understands!
Veterans in transition:

★ Figure out who you are, what you bring to the party, and how you define success.

★ Partner with mentors/advisors to guide you.

★ Learn what employers seek and how they speak (remember — you are joining their world).

People hire people. Automated systems (like online applications) screen people out.
Do yourself a favor — NETWORK, NETWORK, NETWORK.

31

Focus forward. Your past is your launchpad. Honor it; bring lessons learned but focus on the future — because that's where employers are.

We are considering/interviewing you to fill a job and get things done in the future. Focus on this.

We'll ask about your past, your education, your experience, etc., but be aware that what we're listening for is how you take all that great stuff and leverage it to answer our needs and positively impact our future.

If we sense that you are living in the past, focused on making our world the same as the world you came from, or simply not capable of connecting your capabilities with our opportunities, we'll move on to another candidate.

32

If you tell us **I'll do anything,** *we have nothing for you.*

"I can do anything." As true as it may be, it is a meaningless statement. It is also one of the fastest ways to turn off a network contact, a recruiter, or an employer.

Employers don't post "anything" jobs. Their needs are specific.

Similarly, most people in your transition environment want to help. However, they are not able to help if you aren't clear on what you seek.

Get clear on your target. Early. It may shift over time but at least have some idea of what you seek. When people ask what you are looking for, tell them!

I get it. You don't want to limit your opportunities by being too specific. You also may not know what jobs are out there in the civilian world. But unless you have some clarity to share with your network connections, their ability and desire to help you are nearly non-existent.

33

Certifications and degrees may or may not matter. Do your homework before you spend tons of money. You may be better off hiring a coach/advisor.

"To degree or not to degree, that is the question..." The answer matters and has significant potential impact, positives and negatives. It's a sticky wicket with no absolute answers.

I'll suggest:

★ The first question is "What do you want to do?"

★ Next, "What is required to do it?"

★ Followed by "Why do I want to do it?" and "What is the cost/benefit, in terms I value?"

STORY

I knew I needed a bachelor's degree to be a commissioned officer. Done.

I knew I needed a master's degree to be promoted to Major. Done.

At transition, I knew I wanted to get into the HR/talent management field. Degrees required. Done.

I always wanted a PhD. Financial security for my family was my driving priority.

I did the math...a PhD didn't make sense for me.

I'm not a skilled welder. I'm not looking to be a welder. I didn't waste money on a welding certificate.

Some jobs require degrees. Some require certifications. Sometimes experience can substitute for either.

BUT employers often require degrees and/or certifications as entry tickets to the party, and it is their right to do so.

Invest in yourself. Make the time to decide what you want to do. Learn what it takes to get there. Decide what's important to you. Take action with eyes open for atypical opportunities.

34

We look for people with "A's" — Aspiration, Ability, Availability, Agility, and Action.

Of the many ways employers become convinced you are the right person for their job, they often look at what I call the "Five A's."

Many of their questions will center around these to dig beneath the surface and better understand you. The Five A's are pretty common when considering people for opportunities. Military recruiting does something very similar. College and professional sports teams do so also. Executive outplacement, career coaches, and a host of others all consider Aspiration, Ability, Availability, Agility, and Action as part of their work helping others optimize their performance and careers.

★ *Aspiration:* Your focus and desire for both current and long-term employment and growth.

★ *Ability:* The experience, and technical and behavioral capabilities you bring relative to the job requirements.

★ *Availability:* When you will be available to take the job/ join the team. If too late they won't wait.

★ *Agility:* How able are you to adjust to the company culture, tempo, and expectations? Can you honor your past without being a prisoner to it?

★ *Action:* Do you understand what actions are appropriate to the purpose and are you willing/able to take those actions?

It's important to remember:

Aspiration is one thing — wanting it alone doesn't get it.

Ability alone won't land you the job.

Availability — yours must generally match the employer's needs.

Agility is critical in transition — but there's a fine line between "agile" and "scattered."

Action: Action that is focused on purpose, that's the ticket!

Note: "Activity" is not on this list. Motion is not progress. Be sure everything you do is adding value.

35

Confidence and competence are two different things. You need and must balance both.

The people we select to fill our open roles must be both confident and competent.

These are two entirely different things and you must balance them well.

As veterans, you've learned the value of both. Doing tough jobs in strange/hostile places requires both. The military does a great job of developing your competence and confidence. Rigorous training simulating real-world conditions is common.

That said, when you make your career transition, you are entering an entirely new world, one for which there is little training other than what you put in place.

Let's focus on "confidence." It is critical that you understand how impactful striking the right balance is.

For starters, I'll suggest that confidence and humility are different sides of the same saber, with the common theme being "value of perspective."

The balance is how much one values their own perspective versus others' perspectives.

- ★ Value your own too much, you go overboard on "confidence" and trip over to "arrogance."

- ★ Value others' far more than your own and "humility" becomes a hindrance to your value-add.

Unfortunately, there is no magic, mathematical solution to the balance, and the balance is different for every person in every situation. Be aware of it. Be aware of your surroundings. Be agile. Be confident. Don't go overboard.

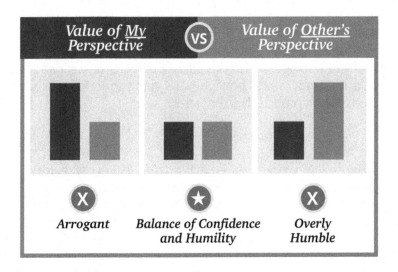

36

Our needs trump your ego. Our egos will get in our way.

Egos are real. A bit of ego is necessary to be successful, especially in tough situations. Unfortunately, too much ego can be a problem.

We expect candidates to come with confidence. We need confident, competent folks on our teams.

That said, when networking, interviewing etc., my ears are perked up for signs that your ego is outweighing my needs. If I get the sense that you are more focused on you than on my needs, a red flag will go up and your appeal as a candidate goes down.

Similarly, sometimes my ego may get in the way. I know what I know about my business, my team, my needs. I likely don't know much about your military background. If my ego is too big, my willingness to listen to your story, understand your perspective, and consider your potential as a top candidate may get in the way of your success.

If you find yourself in this situation, focus on my needs. Help me understand how you are going to help me succeed. Clearly, concisely, completely.

STORY

I once interviewed a top-notch veteran for a critical position on a sales management team. On paper, this gentleman had all the right stuff. Shortly after the interview began it was clear that he was most interested in what we could do for him. His words and demeanor made it clear that we were quite blessed to have the opportunity to even chat with him. His ego was off the charts. I gave him multiple opportunities to shift gears and refocus his perspective to convincing me that he was the best candidate to do the work we need done, and to fit well and add value to our team. He never got it; nor did he get the job.

37

Life ain't fair. Who you know makes a difference. You may be the best candidate but if the CEO wants his friend's nephew, that's what we get.

'Nuff said...

CULTURE

38

A culture gap divides military veterans and the civilian work world. It is significant and solvable.

As I've worked with individual veterans, businesses, and others, it's clear that there is a culture gap dividing military veterans and the civilian work world. This gap is significant and SOLVABLE!

It often seems that military veterans are standing on one shore, with all their great skills, experience, and capabilities, seeking to join employers and add great value.

Employers stand on the other shore — always seeking top talent, always looking for people and ways to improve business.

The culture gap is a giant churning sea that stands between them. Keeping each from the other.

Despite this, there is a strong case for the positive potential of military veteran employment:

★ IF business leaders and their talent managers are truly looking to upgrade diversity, leadership, and overall talent capability, and are willing to better understand veterans.

★ AND military veterans are willing and able to adapt their great capabilities to the civilian work environment.

Work cultures vary from industry to industry, and company to company. Some are more like the military than not (e.g., law enforcement, some defense contractors) while others are wildly different (e.g., some high-tech firms, advertising, and marketing firms etc.). They are neither better nor worse, but they are very different.

As you transition, do your homework. Research industries, companies, careers, and positions. Seek informational interviews. Pay attention to other people. Watch their mannerisms, posture, intensity, directness, and similar non-verbal cues — their presence. Thoughtfully consider your own non-verbals, your presence. Ask others to describe it to you. If your presence is not well aligned with those around you, you may not be in the right place. It's better to figure this out during transition, search, and interviewing than once you've landed.

STORY

I heard of a veteran who landed an operations manager job at a manufacturing plant. The particulars of manufacturing were new to this gentleman but the owner was confident he had the right leadership skills and experience to do the work that needed to be done. Things started out well. People responded positively to the veteran's solid, positive, energetic, focused presence. They loved that he was clear in his communication and straightforward in his dealings. He was able to make value-adding impact early on. As often happens, each win created positive momentum, generating more and more wins. Operational performance was improving and most of the teams were also improving. One day several of the veteran's colleagues approached him. Although he always presented himself with supreme professionalism and he was getting great results, these folks were ticked off. It seems they were upset that he was generating so many wins and moving so quickly. You see they were experienced, long-tenured managers. They liked the way things used to be and, moreover, they had never produced to his level or had such success with teams. They told him he was "too powerful," "coming on too strong," and should "strive for mediocrity." He was shocked. Could this really be true? "Strive for mediocrity"? His whole professional career was about excellence. About going above and beyond. The fact of the matter is that our veteran, by his presence, his drive, his initiative, scared these folks. His solid results intimidated them; after all, he didn't come from the industry! How could he possibly be so successful?

Be aware of your environment. Be you but know that if your presence is too different than those around you, egos, politics, resistance, and other negative concerns may pop up on your path to success.

The bridge across the culture gap must be closed from both sides! Certainly, employers have a responsibility to help bridge the gap, but let there be no doubt — as a transitioning veteran, your success is directly impacted by your willingness and ability to acknowledge these gaps, learn about them and their impact, and take action that closes them and/or mitigates their negative potential.

39
Our culture is what it is — not what yours used to be.

Every organization has its own unique culture. Military culture is unique. Inside the military, each service branch's culture is unique. Inside each service branch, every unit's culture is unique.

Service members and veterans are very familiar with military culture. It is ingrained from Day 1. It is imparted in basic training and reinforced through your career. Whether or not you liked it, it has an impact on you.

Culture in the civilian work world is every bit as impactful. In most organizations, it is very different than the military. There is likely little formal "culture" training, which leaves employees to learn it on their own, on the job.

While different, be assured it is every bit as impactful on people. As I've mentioned several times already, employers are looking for people who can do the work they need done and who will FIT IN THEIR CULTURE.

40

The "Experience Gap." You haven't experienced ours. We haven't experienced yours. Quite frankly, you are a bit of an outsider trying to break into our world.

As a military veteran, you likely come with little to no experience in the civilian work world. You may have worked in a civilian job before the military, but that was several years (or decades) ago. The job markets have changed. Technology has changed. You have changed. You now come to the employment market with skills, experience, education, and capabilities that can add significant value for the right employers — if you are able to tell your story in a way that makes sense to us.

The other side of this experience gap is on the employer side. Well over 90% of the population has never served in military uniform. Think about that! Nearly everyone around you has zero experience similar to yours! This is not to say employers are bad people or that their experiences are invalid. Quite to the contrary, the civilian work world is replete with bright, capable, experienced, passionate people who make great things happen every day. The vast majority are committed to their jobs and to success.

They do not, however, share your experience. Their perspective is formed through experience in the world you seek to enter. Their experience is no less important than yours.

As a veteran you are a bit of an outsider trying to break into their world. How you go about this matters. No matter how much great capability you think you bring, if you don't figure out how to apply it to the new world, you will come up short.

41

Impact of the Experience Gap?

★ Your background and experience intimidate some of us. It's just too "big" for us to understand.

★ Your combat stories scare many of us.

People fear what they don't know. Just as you find the transition to the civilian work world a bit "scary," civilians sometimes find your experience a bit scary. Think of it. The military is dangerous business. It exists to do big things. For many it includes combat, which is scary stuff all around. Bringing this big, scary stuff to the workplace can be intimidating to the unaware.

STORY

Several years ago, I was a panelist at a networking meeting for salaried professionals in career transition. Of the 30-some people in the room one stood out. A U.S. Army colonel, dressed perfectly in his blues. Highly decorated and with the typically impressive presence one might

> *expect, he got noticed even before speaking. The range of response was startling. A couple of us were veterans and wondered why he showed up at this event in military uniform (we all assumed, correctly, that he came direct from a work function.) Most of the folks were unfamiliar and curious (they knew he was military but didn't know anything more). Some of the folks were immediately and obviously upset that he was there. The presence of someone in the military was very much against their preference, experience, comfort level, and willingness to accept. As often happens in these forums, each participant was asked to introduce themselves and tell a bit about their background and recent work. When this colonel's turn came, he spoke as you might expect — clear, concise, complete, direct — about his work on "national strategic countermeasure planning for nuclear, biological, radiological mass attacks on our homeland." You could feel the air leave the room. The nature and scope of what he described was so far beyond what most others ever conceived, that they all recoiled. They were scared.*

Be aware of your surroundings. Read your audience. Remember most don't have your experience. Focus your message so it is well received and helps you move forward.

42

No matter how much great capability you think you bring, if you don't figure out how to apply it to the new world, you will come up short.

As a military veteran, you bring a great capability to the civilian work world. You've been trained in some of the most complex, dangerous areas of human life. You're familiar with highly sophisticated, cutting-edge technology. You've experienced challenging, meaningful work in broadly diverse global environments with amazingly diverse people.

But so what? How does that apply to what employers need?

Use that great "agility" that veterans are famous for. Learn what employers need. Figure out how your capabilities address employer needs. Learn how to explain it to employers in a way we can understand.

43

We don't have uniforms per se. It impacts how we interact/operate/make decisions.

Unless you transition to some manner of uniformed service (e.g., police, fire, other first responders) most jobs have no uniform. They may have a dress code (e.g., business, business casual) but none of these include wearing your resume on your shirt.

Think about this example:

As a military service member, you've recently arrived at a new duty station. You are attending your first staff meeting. You know no one. As people enter the room, name tags make it easy to identify who's who. Rank insignia informs you as to who "fits" where, and who likely has responsibility and authority for what. Badges, awards, and other appurtenances give you quick, valuable insight as to their past — their resume is on display! Within moments you get a workable knowledge of who's who, how they fit, the potential value they may bring, who's likely to discuss what, who are the "recommenders" and who are the "deciders."

Now let's switch gears. You're now in the civilian work world. You've just landed your dream job. You've completed your onboarding, found your workspace, the coffee pot and the restrooms (yes "restroom"...not "head," "latrine," or other). You arrive at your first team meeting and see that most people are wearing clothing appropriate for the dress code (well, except maybe a couple folks but since you're not really sure what "business casual" means, maybe they are). You grab a seat at the conference table as others stream in. You've not met anyone. No name tags. No identifiable markings on their clothing. A few folks say "Hi." Some greet you with their first name. Suddenly someone says, "let's begin". The meeting starts and you have no idea who's who. Who brings what expertise to the discussion? Who is the top dog? Who's voice matters? Suddenly you're not focused on the meeting's purpose/topic, you're just trying to keep up with the discussion while earnestly trying to figure out who's who.

The point is the lack of uniform has an impact. Uniforms remove many distractions. They provide information that enables even new team members to effectively contribute sooner. Without uniforms people spend time and energy getting familiar with the players, the structure, the organization, the key issues, and so many other topics, and their initial contributions are delayed/diminished. For the record, I am not suggesting employers adopt uniforms but I am suggesting veterans be aware of the difference before walking into that conference room!

44

Our sense of purpose is different.
Many veterans find it lacking.

Everyone wants a purpose. Everyone needs a purpose. We all want to know that we are contributing to something worthwhile, that the effort we expend is adding to something meaningful.

As veterans, we get this. We have a sense of service. A sense of purpose. Paraphrasing President Ronald Reagan, "Some people live an entire lifetime and wonder if they have ever made a difference in the world. The veteran doesn't have that problem."

While many organizations are great examples of "purpose," for many it is little more than a poster on the wall: ink on paper that adorns offices and meeting rooms, rarely applied in a coherent manner to policies, programs, or practices; infrequently seen in action; bastardized by misaligned leaders, managers and employees who are more focused on their particular priorities, wants, or needs.

This particular culture gap can be brutal for a veteran to face. In fact, this has been the single most prevalent concern I've heard over the years from veterans who have landed in civilian jobs.

The added dimension here is that if you as a veteran come in too hard on this (or other gaps) you run the risk of your bosses and other counterparts thinking you are "calling their baby ugly" — unjustly criticizing their culture, reinforcing the stereotype that veterans are too direct, hard, or other, and thus you place yourself in a potentially risky spot.

If you find yourself in this position, put on your best leadership hat and help be part of the solution working within the culture to help evolve it.

45

Near-universal support for you, your job, and your mission does not exist.

Veterans come to the civilian work world from a mission-driven culture. Everything in the military is about mission and mission success: The way people are inducted, training, organization, resourcing, communications, decision-making, facilities, and equipment, base support, family support, healthcare...everything exists to ensure the mission is successfully accomplished. This support is not only for some abstract, overarching mission of the top-level organization (e.g., The Army, Big Navy); it is about you, your team, your organization, etc. Everything is designed (even if not always well executed) for your mission success.

The civilian work environment is generally much less mission focused. Mission, purpose, strategy, etc. may not be robustly developed, articulated, or communicated. Different departments, teams, functions may not be well aligned. Individual understanding of these may vary wildly. As you might imagine, this creates an entirely different environment, one with innumerable challenges and opportunities. It is not inherently bad but it is often dramatically different than the military and it is a culture gap that you must be aware of.

Certainly, there are great examples of organizations that are superbly mission focused and capable but many are not. This lack of unified support and mission focus is often cited as one of the major challenges veterans encounter when they first enter the civilian work world.

Having awareness of this gap, you can assess how you may refine your search and approach the topic if/when it comes up while networking, interviewing, or on the job.

46

Communication practices often are not as formalized as the military. Language, formats, expectations, nature, frequency, channels, and other considerations may be unclear and variable.

The military has well-developed communication practices. From the basic phonetic alphabet to highly formatted, standardized estimates, orders, reports, updates, and others, the rigor of military communications enables those trained in them to focus primarily on the content, its meaning, impact, and so forth, rather than on distracting concerns like, "How do I say this?" "How do I read it?" "Who sent it?" "Is it important?" etc.

Of course, communications of all types exist in the civilian work world. Some rival the military. Some are well established and highly effective. These are typically found at larger or more established companies (although great examples may also be found at smaller, newer firms also).

Several common communication-related notes:

★ **Nearly no one speaks "Mil-speak" or "Veteran-ese"** — which makes sense since over 90% of people never served in uniform.

★ **Different acronyms, phrasing unique to the company/industry are common (which can be as complex as Mil-speak).** The military does not hold exclusive rights to acronyms. Every organization has its own unique shorthand and acronyms that can be every bit as pervasive and complex as the military's. Most employers won't expect you to know these on Day 1, but they do expect you to drop the Mil-speak and begin learning/using their language ASAP.

★ **Few established formats** — The military has a form, template, model, or format for everything. Not so in many civilian companies, where these are often created, developed, revised, and employed in a much more local, ad hoc basis.

EXAMPLE

For example, let's suppose Finance works with all the business leaders to create and deploy a revenue capture report. It does exactly what finance needs it to do. The top-level leaders all agree to it. After the first round of use, a controller or analyst somewhere decides that they need the report to do something more, less, or different, to really answer their business needs. So, they "enhance" the report and submit something more, less, or different than everyone else and different than what finance expected.

This can lead to all manner of problems that then must be dealt with to ensure data quality, integrity, and timeliness.

★ **Unclear/frequently changing information expectations** — "Change is the only constant." We've all heard this phrase. As military veterans we've lived and worked in fluid, dynamic, ever-changing environments. Once in the civilian work world, we are agile and typically face these situations with professional aplomb — after all, nobody's shooting at us. We are also familiar with having a lack of information and we know how to deal with it. The largest gap here is the lack of clarity regarding expectations. It's not often that military members don't know what the mission is, what "good is supposed to look like," or what the "commander's intent" is. Even when the environment is fluid, when we don't have all the information, if we have clarity regarding expectations, we will find a way through. Oftentimes, civilian organizations are challenged with this clarity, knowing/obtaining optimal information, and dealing with change. As a veteran you have great potential to help, but only if the organization is ready for help and you provide it in a manner that doesn't "call their baby ugly."

★ **Unspecified distributions (leading to the use of "information as power")** — The military's rigorous distribution and routing practices help make dissemination of information to the right people, in the right format, at the right time fairly easy. Figuring out who to include ("cc," "bcc," or other) in the civilian workforce can be quite ambiguous. This creates the risk of the right people missing information and the wrong people getting info they don't need or shouldn't be bothered with. At the very least it creates noise, confusion, and delays. At worst, ill-intended folks may use this to leverage their personal agendas, recognizing that info is power and then selectively including or excluding folks who rightly should/shouldn't have the information.

47
Decisions aren't always rational.

By and large, decision-making in the military is based around the rational decision-making approach, which focuses on logic more than emotion and uses a structured approach to make the best possible decisions. There is much value to this. It is also used in the civilian work world.

That said, there is a much higher prevalence of "non-rational decision-making" in the civilian world. Non-rational decision-making assumes more focus on emotion, less-than-perfect information, less time, less knowledge, and it is often conducted in a less structured manner.

This inherently is neither good nor bad, better or worse, nor more or less valid than rational decision-making, but it is different. Being aware of this difference can help a veteran manage through or overcome areas where decisions are being taken in an unfamiliar manner. It may even offer the veteran an opportunity to help the organization improve how they make decisions.

48

Career management isn't the same.

★ It is not nearly as robust.

★ Nobody cares more about your career than you do.

★ I'll promote who I want — even if you think they're dumb-asses.

Career management in the military is robust. From initial entry through basic training, professional development schools, specialty schools, various qualification programs, and so many others, the military is unrivaled when it comes to career management.

Whether an E1, W1, or O1, you know every step it takes to make 2, then 3, and so on. You know the general timing, the schools, the assignments that are helpful. The career path is crystal clear.

This is because the military must develop its talent — or "build" it. Other than initial entry (and a very few select professional specialties) the military can't go out and recruit ("buy") talent to fill gaps in the middle/top ranks. Thus, the military's approach to career management has evolved and developed over generations, improving along the way and continuing to produce highly capable service members and leaders to handle our nation's security today and tomorrow.

The civilian work world, however, has two options to obtain the talent capability it needs. It can build it or buy it. Building it, similar to the military, takes a significant investment of time, money, and resources. Businesses often see these expenses more as costs and resource drains than value-adding investments. Thus, they choose not to build. Instead, they often buy their talent — recruiting and hiring from outside the company to fill middle/top positions. They seek people who can do the work they need done and that will fit in and add value to their culture. They look for folks with a proven track record of success, who's performance in similar roles and situations is outstanding. They want people who can hit the ground running and can make an immediate positive impact. They look to the general employment market, their competitors, their suppliers, even their customers.

This is important to know for a couple reasons.

One, you need to know that your competition will be tough. There will be candidates who have been successful in jobs and industries substantially similar to the opening you seek to fill. They will be attractive to the employer.

The other reason this is important to know is that we, as veterans, are used to our roles changing frequently, always offering new experience, adding to our capability portfolio, and readying us for ever-more senior roles. This is not the case in most civilian companies. You are hired to do a job. There may or may not be opportunity to grow. The formal, rigorous processes you experienced in the military likely are nowhere to be found. Rather, you may find that six months down the road you are being asked to take on a different (maybe bigger) job. You may also find that three years after landing this gig, you are still doing the same job and are getting antsy for more challenge, only to be told that you are too valuable in your current role to move. You may find that a plumb assignment you have longed for was suddenly filled by someone else (who happened to be connected to a key decision-maker). Career management truly is different in the civilian world. You need to be aware of the difference.

STORY

A highly capable young army officer contacted me one day. He was transitioning to the civilian job market, seeking a project management role in the energy industry, specifically nuclear power. He had great, relevant experience in the military. By all accounts he should have been an attractive candidate. As we chatted, he shared that he had received an offer for a position very similar to his target. I congratulated him and asked how I could help. He advised that he thought the offered salary was a bit low. He knew the employer was not going to budge on that, so he inquired about his potential career path. The employer responded that he was being hired to do this job and that if he performed well opportunities may arise in the future. That didn't sit well with this young officer, who pressed for details. He wanted to know the 6-, 12-, 18-, and 24-month career plan. The employer again advised that future roles were unknown. The young officer pressed again, clearly touching a nerve with the employer, who at this point simply rescinded the offer. Career management is different, and no matter what you are used to, you are going to a new world and will have to adapt.

49
Results matter, not effort.
'Nuff said ...

50

Hurry up and wait isn't just a military thing.

Just like when you were at basic training and had to hurry up and wait, there is a reason, whether you know it or not, and whether you like it or not.

Customer change, vendor change, material availability, myriad other causes, sometimes we wait. Every wait is money down the drain.

The transition process, networking, recruiting, interview, and selection will all go slower than you'd like. Same for employers. That said, there are numerous variables in play of which you will have no knowledge.

Be patient. Be thoughtful. Don't take rash actions that might hinder your success.

51

People are our most important asset...they are also expendable.

While in the Army I learned the phrase "Mission first — people always." It's a great reminder that we must get the work done and that work only gets done with people. Balancing these two critical truths is at the heart of leadership.

Military leaders must make hard decisions that sometimes puts people in harm's way. Some missions are critical and deadly. Some of our brave servicemembers pay the ultimate price.

In the civilian work world, organizations are often heard to say, "People are our greatest asset." No doubt it is true in many organizations and many people believe it. While it can be true, most civilian jobs do not require employees to give their life to achieve their objectives.

That said, sometimes organizations must make decisions that reduce headcount. Perhaps business conditions changed and costs must be cut. Often the solution with the fastest, biggest savings is to eliminate jobs. Get used to it. It is what it is.

52

Your former rank means nothing to most of us.

Private? Petty Officer? Sergeant? Major? Sergeant Major? Rear Admiral? Lieutenant General?

What in the world does all this mean? Why is it such a big deal?

Look, most employers have no idea what ranks, rates, grades, MOS, AFSCs, or any of the other related titles mean. They haven't experienced the military and have had no reason to learn such things.

Furthermore, employers all use job titles differently. Sure, there are some typical patterns (supervisor, manager, director, vice president, president, etc.) but there are no hard-and-fast rules that correlate titles across businesses. A manager at a large, complex, global company may have a much larger scope than a vice president at a smaller firm. The "account executive" title may be used at one company as an entry level sales job or as a top-level sales leader in another. A human resource (HR) business partner may be a first level role at one company or a top-level leadership job at another.

If you're impressed with your former rank/title, get over it. Figure out what jobs interest you, how the jobs stack up in particular organizations, what value you bring to those jobs, and how you are going to be the most attractive candidate to fill that job.

53

Performance management — not what you are used to.

Unfortunately, employers often don't set clear goals. Feed-back quality and timeliness varies greatly. Performance re-view discussions may or may not happen and may or may not be meaningful. Many people in positions of authority have no performance management training or experience. The focus/purpose of performance management is often little more than to provide input to a compensation plan-ning model.

Yep, quite different than what you are used to. Set your expectations accordingly.

54

Leadership *is often a position title — not a capability, characteristic, perspective, or set of behaviors.*

One of the most impactful cultural differences between the military and civilian work world is leadership. Far too often:

★ *Leadership* refers to little more than a position title.

★ The duties/activities/responsibilities, etc. that veter-ans know as leadership are foreign concepts to peo-ple in positions of authority.

★ Management activities are thought to be leadership.

While these and similar differences can present a chal-lenge to veterans in the civilian workplace, they also offer opportunity...opportunity to help organizations extend their success by learning and adopting improved leadership capabilities.

STORY

Several years ago — when I was the senior talent management leader for a large, complex, global company — the CEO tasked me to build a "leadership development strategy and program." This was a great assignment, one that I knew could add real value to the organization both in terms of business results and company culture. As you might imagine there were many deliverables, many variables, and much work to be done to even get this important project out of the starting gate. As I assessed the situation and began setting priorities and building my plan, I realized there was only one possible first step — to answer THE core question "How does the leadership team define leadership?" This proved to be a much more difficult challenge than you might first think. We spent weeks working together defining, refining, considering, collaborating, and finally agreeing on just what leadership means. From there we were able to do great value-adding work that truly did make a positive impact on business results and culture.

STORY

"Person in a Position of Authority" (PIPA) ... we've all met them. They fill a seat.

They wear the title.

PIPAs aren't leaders.

PIPAs aren't managers.

They rely on the title to drive activity.

They offer platitudes as false attempts to motivate.

They abdicate in the name of delegation.

They eat first, take the glory, and deflect blame.

If you happen to have the honor of filling a position of authority, realize it is a responsibility — not a reward.

Manage things effectively.

Lead people genuinely.

Don't be a PIPA.

55

We're not going to give you time at work to search for your next job.

Transitioning out of the military often includes your command making time available for you to attend the TAP and do the work you need to do to prepare for your transition. There are even opportunities where you may be able to take on an internship with a civilian company rather than perform your regular duties (e.g., Department of Defense's SkillBridge and similar programs).

Take advantage of every opportunity possible. Make good use of the time and resources because they are unique.

Precious few employers or circumstances exist where you are allowed to use company time and/or company resources to search/prepare for your next job/career. Why would we? We are paying you to do the work we need done and to be a value-adding part of OUR team — not some other team.

56

Office politics are real. They can be a dangerous game to play. Know them but don't play them.

Yes, office politics exist in the military, but I'll suggest that they are far more prevalent and impactful in the civilian work world.

Personal agendas, power grabs, immature attempts to undermine others, and so many other negative motivators impact work life.

Be aware that these exist. Understand that they have an impact. BUT — don't play the game. Rise above them. Focus on the work that needs to be done. Leverage your professional military and leadership experience. Set a positive example. Be part of the solution and not part of the problem.

Politics may be part of the interview and selection process. You likely will not know if they exist, their root cause, or their impact. Don't get hung up on it. Network effectively to build the best possible connections and relationships. Be professional. Present yourself well. The chips will fall where they fall. You likely will never know what went on behind the curtain.

57

Don't expect to come in as the CEO.

What may appear to be a step back/setback may just be a launchpad for something great. Remember, an arrow doesn't leave the bow until after it is drawn back...

TRANSITION

58

Transition is a journey...arguably one of the most challenging change management experiences a person might have.

For the last several years (or perhaps decades) you have lived and worked in a very specific environment, one that has provided you tremendous experience, development, challenge, opportunity, and many great capabilities. As you end that phase of life, you look forward to your next phase, your next job/career.

Standing between you and that next career is the transition.

It is a particular thing, a unique environment that has little in common with your past, and quite frankly, not everything in common with your future. It truly is a transition, a period of change, a unique, transient experience.

While it is common for people to want to skip right to the next job/career, doing so without preparing for, learning about, and becoming skilled at 'transitioning' makes landing well in that new job/career exponentially more difficult.

Taking time to learn all you can about the transition environment and the talent acquisition environment is a critical investment that will pay immeasurable dividends toward optimizing your career success.

Starting early in your career makes transition easier. It truly is an investment in yourself and your future, where your small efforts over time accumulate knowledge, develop networks, enable a value-adding perspective, and become an "evergreen," living plan.

STORY

Jonny decides now is the time to rebuild his deck. It is a totally new challenge. He's not a carpenter, has never done similar work before, and has no idea what he wants the deck to look like. He has no network of skilled craftsmen to tap in to. He spends hours and days working on the deck. Several weeks later he's tired, frustrated, and looking at a monstrosity of wood and nails that in no way resembles a deck. He blames his toolbox. It was too small. It didn't have the right tools in it. The lid wouldn't stay open, etc. He wonders just exactly what went wrong!

The fact is, he failed to recognize the magnitude of this new challenge. He didn't know what he needed to know about the task, proper tools, design, and construction topics, etc., and he didn't build or employ a network of folks who could help, coach, or advise before he dove in.

He busted his tail and wound up with a result he never anticipated — and didn't much like.

Transition is like this. Resources are available if you seek them. They help you if you learn how to use them. None of them will get you where you want to be if you have no idea where you want to be.

1. Define who you are and what you bring to the party.

2. Define success.

3. Understand your transition environment.

(BTW, refinishing a 600-square-foot deck with a 3-inch hand belt sander is NOT the way to go ...)

59

Military and civilian work-world cultures are vastly different.

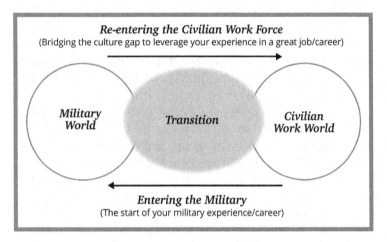

When you entered the military, whether via basic training, boot camp, a service academy, ROTC, direct commission, or another start point, you made a transition from your civilian life to the military. This was a very structured process with well-established practices. It has evolved for generations under the watchful eyes of military leaders that understand the critical importance of onboarding and initial training. You endured tremendous training and experiences that at their root did two things:

★ Taught you how to do the work that needs to be done.

★ Trained you how to fit in the culture.

Before you shipped for initial entry, rigorous testing and assessment were done to identify what job/career field you qualified for. Your options were then limited based on the needs of your service branch.

Perhaps you signed on to be a Navy Avionics Technician but once you got to boot camp, the needs of the Navy changed. You no longer had that job available to you. So, you had a couple choices. Experts were available to help you understand the options and then at some point you made your decision, likely selecting another option for which there was also rigorous training and a structured career path.

Perhaps you participated in ROTC. Your branch of choice was Infantry but the needs of the Army only made Ordnance available; so it goes. Your service was training you to "fit" and preparing you to do the work it needed done.

60

The transition into the military was much more structured than your transition out.

Fast-forward to the end of your military service. You are now making another transition. The transition back to the civilian world. This time, however, you are not going into a highly structured organization, with fantastic overall mission clarity, unified focus, and generations of experience selecting, developing and employing people to get the work done and fit in the culture.

You are now leaving that environment and entering a world of nearly innumerable options; vastly different approaches to everything; amazingly variable purposes, processes, products, people, structures, approaches, levels of rigor — and about any other factor you could imagine.

This transition is significantly different. You come to it with valuable, deeply ingrained experiences, skills, perspectives, and so on. There is no recruiting station for you to check in with, there is no robust basic training that provides you everything you'll need to make it across the culture gap. While there are numerous resources available to help with whatever your particular focus area might be, for the first time in years you are now truly on your own facing an unfamiliar "battlefield" with only your experience, perspective, capabilities, and the support you are able to gather and deploy against a culture gap with which you likely are quite unfamiliar.

61

Transition is a space of its own — a "career battlefield," if you will.

It resides between your past and your future: between the military culture you come from and the new civilian work culture to which you aspire.

The graphic below displays what I call the *Career Battlefield* as a means to depict transition and help explain the various key parts of its three operating spaces.

Transition is not a pass through. It is a complex environment with many moving parts, all of which need to be well understood to optimize your transition success and subsequent success in the civilian work world.

There are three operating spaces on the career battlefield.

★ You and your prior career.

★ The transition environment.

★ The talent acquisition environment.

As you move from left to right, the work culture shifts from the military (with which you are quite familiar) to the civilian (with which most veterans are quite unfamiliar). *Remember — the vast majority of civilians never served in the*

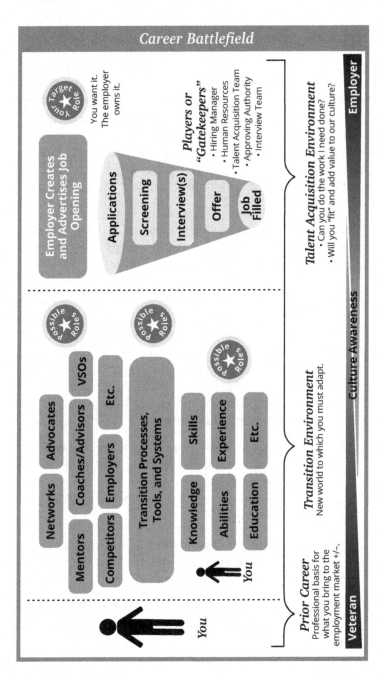

military and have little to no familiarity with the world from which you come.

On the left is you and your prior career. It is the "launch pad for your transition." It provided you with experience, skills, perspective, and other capabilities and characteristics that are potentially value-adding for employers. It also created some blind spots and areas you will need to develop to understand the world you are about to enter, and to help employers in that world understand how you will add value to their business.

In the middle is the transition environment. This is a new world unto itself, one that you must successfully navigate to eventually land in a job/career you desire.

★ At the base, are the capabilities you bring to transition and the employment market — your knowledge, skills, abilities, experience, and education. The bulk of these are garnered through your prior work history but be mindful that, as you go through transition, you will learn. These learnings add to your "tool kit" and become capabilities that you must recognize and use to gain leverage in your search.

★ There are also multiple new players with whom you will have to get familiar. Networks, advocates, mentors, coaches, advisors, employers, competitors, and a bevy of veteran service organizations and other supportive individuals.

★ New resources, processes, tools, and systems exist in the transition environment, some of which you may be familiar with; others you may never have heard of.

★ There are also likely to be potential jobs that pop up throughout your transition. Some will come before you are ready; some will appear but not be a fit for you. There might even be a fantastic, perfect fit that arises. The key here is to have your eyes and ears open; learn as much as you can about yourself, transition, and the opportunity; and NOT make any decisions prematurely or out of sheer desperation.

On the right is the talent acquisition environment. This is where the work of getting that job you really want happens, where you employ everything you've learned and done so far. This is the world that includes the nuts and bolts of how jobs get filled in the civilian employment marketplace. The work you do in the Transition phase prepares you for success here (and beyond). Optimizing your experience here is a function of how familiar you are with the people and processes, AND how well you did your work in the transition environment.

62

Career transition falls between two worlds and is a thoroughly different world unto itself.

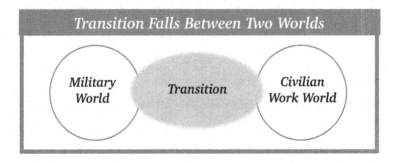

Transition Falls Between Two Worlds

Military World   Transition   Civilian Work World

63

You are now entering an open field, one with which you likely are not so familiar.

The choices, challenges, opportunities, and obstacles in front of you now are nearly endless. It is exciting. It is scary. It will require new decisions that you've likely never had to make before, and these decisions will impact the rest of your life.

Typical paths for most transitioning veterans include:

★ Joining an existing civilian company or organization as an employee.

★ Buying into a franchise.

★ Entrepreneurship — starting your own new business.

★ Education.

★ Full retirement.

There are many great stories of huge successes in all these paths. All come with pros/cons, challenges, and opportunities. Think carefully about your path before you jump onto it.

64

As a transitioning veteran job seeker, you have much to do.

Transitioning from the military requires focus and attention in many areas — exiting the service properly, preparing for the next phase of life, taking care of your family, etc. You will have to make some hard decisions.

Relative to your job-seeker efforts, quite simply, you are seeking employment. Whether a job or a career, you are looking for employment.

This workstream includes a vast array of topics, actions, and other aspects that require your time, attention, focus, and effort. It may seem daunting, but you have succeeded in daunting situations before. Leverage your experience. Learn. Prepare. Plan. Execute. You will succeed here too!

What you've been doing for the last few years (or decades) is now in your rear-view mirror. That past shaped who you are today, your perspective on life, and your capabilities, but the future is in front of you — not in the past.

65

Start preparing now, even if transition is years away. Like investing for retirement, small "deposits" over time accumulate and grow compound interest.

Every service member knows the uniform is going to come off someday and they will face career transition. It only makes sense to start thinking about it now. It doesn't have to be a big daily task.

Start by simply thinking of what you want to do after the military. Learn a bit about these jobs/careers: what they actually do; what they require; who hires them; what they pay; etc.

Every little bit of work you do and information you gather puts you one step further ahead for transition success. Every bit of this work also helps to create positive momentum that will serve you well when transition does arrive.

66

Just like pilots — who must keep "eyes on the dials" and "eyes on the horizon" — always keep a dual focus on 1. Getting prepared 2. Getting known.

- ★ Getting prepared is all about making sure you learn and do as much as possible to be ready for transition before it arrives.

- ★ Getting known is all about making sure employers and others know that:

  - ★ You are looking for opportunities.

  - ★ You are in transition.

  - ★ You have good stuff that will add value to their business.

67

Your military career shaped you. It is the launchpad for your future. Figure out how to leverage it to meet employers' needs.

Some of what you learned directly applies to the civilian work world. Some of it won't. That said, how you think, make decisions, take action, and so many other valuable capabilities have all been shaped by your military experience. You may not be able to employ them directly in your transition and future job/career but they are certainly part of who you are. Leverage them. Make good use of them to enable a successful transition and future career.

68

Mentors, coaches, and advisors are key to your learning — engage them.

Mentors, coaches, and advisors are folks with whom you engage that provide value-adding perspective, insights, or information on your transition or other professional topics that help optimize your success. They may already be part of your network or they may become part of it as you expand it.

Mentors are experienced, trusted advisors, typically more tenured in the topic, area, and environment you are targeting. Mentors offer broad and deep insight for you to consider and use as you best see fit. Mentorships are a safe, typically long-term relationship focused on developing the mentee for the future, with no set agenda. Mentors add value by passing along their knowledge and experience. When considering a mentor, be open to different ideas. While mentors tend to be more tenured folks, that doesn't necessarily mean older. There are many great examples of "reverse mentoring," in which younger people are providing value-adding mentorship to older colleagues in a variety of topic areas including technology and generational awareness to name a few. You will also do well to consider mentors from outside your current industry or career field. If your focus is on career transition, connecting with a mentor that is skilled there likely will be quite valuable.

Coaches are most commonly instructors or trainers. They help you better understand and perform certain skills and capabilities, and improve performance. The relationships tend to be structured to help set and meet certain goals, understand and overcome challenges, and enhance growth in particular areas. Coaches don't necessarily have all the answers but they do bring an outside, pragmatic perspective that adds real value.

Advisors are folks that provide advice and guidance in specific areas. They work with individuals and organizations to help them answer important questions, make important decisions, and solve important problems.

While each of these are unique and provide different value in different ways, these three terms are often used interchangeably. I've noted the differences here as a general baseline of knowledge to help you better understand the type of service you might seek to address your situation. Don't get too hung up on the semantics — when you find someone that adds value, build the relationship!

You might engage with any of these informally or formally.

Informal engagements are less structured, based on common conversations, and have less-defined objectives. For example, an informal mentor may be someone you know and trust, who you call upon infrequently to bounce ideas off. An informal coach may be a colleague skilled in an area who you occasionally connect with to learn. An informal advisor may be someone in your network or an outsider referred to you by a network connection, who you contact seeking advice on a particular topic of interest. Informal engagements may be conducted for a fee or with no charge.

Formal engagements tend to be more structured, have more defined parameters and expectations, and often are based on a written agreement, statement of work, or contract. Formal engagements often are on a paid basis.

We've all heard the idea that "no one should charge a veteran." Conceptually, I find it hard to disagree. There are literally thousands of providers who offer free mentoring, coaching, advice, and so on to transitioning service members and veterans. Many are fantastic. Sometimes, though, you get what you pay for. There are also for-profit providers that offer our military members and veterans these services. Again, some are great value-add, while others are not. As you enter the civilian, commercial world, investing in yourself and making wise choices about where to spend for your future is important. Look beyond the "free" sign to really understand the potential value. Are the people experienced on both sides of transition? Are they veterans? Did they transition successfully? Do they have relevant experience in a civilian job?

69

Myriad VSOs exist to help you — reach out to them.

There are nearly innumerable VSOs (veteran service organizations) that provide services to veterans. Some are fraternal, social organizations that provide a great place for veterans to come together and share time. Others specialize in certain areas such as healthcare, employment, recreation, and so on. These are generally non-profit groups, and they offer a fantastic array of help to the veteran community. Google them. Check out what they offer. Connect, join, hang around, partake of the services that are most relevant to you. They can add tremendous value to your transition and yourself personally. They also provide potentially fantastic networking opportunities beyond their primary missions that can add real value to your transition. These may include connecting with other veterans to just shoot the breeze, participating in community support activities, and/

or connecting with long-time members who might connect you to others with opportunities in your area.

70

There are hundreds of more qualified candidates for my job than you — with industry experience you don't have.

Your competition is not just military veterans — most will be industry veterans. How will you compete and be the best?

In your military career, you had competition for new jobs, promotions, training opportunities, etc. You all came from the same source and had generally similar development backgrounds, career paths, etc. You may even know some or many of your competitors, especially as you become more senior.

As you enter the transition environment, planning and conducting your transition, learning how to transition, learning about the talent acquisition environment that lies ahead, and ultimately the civilian work world, you will come face-to-face with entirely new competitors — non-military veterans. These are folks who have not walked your path. They don't have your experience or perspective. They don't bring the same value-adding capabilities you do, BUT that doesn't mean they aren't highly capable, attractive candidates for employers' open jobs. In fact, they are likely MORE attractive candidates. They likely come with industry experience, experience in the market(s) the employer seeks to serve, or maybe even have personal connections with people in positions of authority in the company or in their networks. They know the civilian work world — they've been living it the entire time you were in the military. They "speak the language." They understand the nuances that make all the difference. They do not come with the baggage of bias, stereotypes, and preconceived negative notions about military veterans. They are also technical experts with direct experience in the industry, product, function, market, or other areas. There is little need to translate their experience. Recruiters, HR, hiring managers, and others in the chain understand them better than they understand you and, in many cases, very busy people will not take the time or effort to figure you out. They will simply go to a candidate who's easier to understand.

★ Never underestimate your competition.

★ Put in the work. Don't make it easy for your competition by failing to be competitive.

★ As the old saying goes, "The harder you work, the luckier you get."

71

Employers are part of your transition. Get to know us.

While your transition is not any employer's primary concern, we also exist in your "transition environment." Our missions are ongoing, independent of your transition/search. Our job openings come and go as business circumstances dictate. We may have relationships with people or organizations with which you are networking. We may participate in job fairs or other employment-focused events that you attend. Get to know us. Reach out. Establish contact. For those who are relevant to your transition/search, develop that contact into a connection and make us a value-adding part of your network.

72

Where to start your transition work? Framework for career transition success.

When I coach individuals in career transition, I use the pro-prietary model I developed years ago, my "Framework for Career Transition Success." This is a robust, structured, in-teractive process of Definition, Assessment, Decision, and Action that helps optimize job search/career transition by purposely considering critical variables that impact job search/career transition. It includes the following steps:

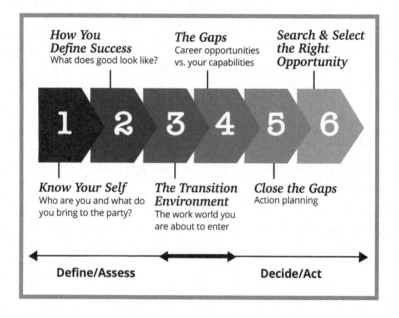

This is a linear process that builds your capability. Far too often people skip right to the last step, searching blind-ly for some undefined target, not knowing who they are, what they seek, how to plan for and engage with the vari-ous new people, processes, etc. they will face or how they will know if they've won once they find a target.

1. Start with you — Who are you and what do you bring to the party? What are you good at? What do you want to do? What qualifies you to do these things? What is your family situation? Finances? Where do you want to work? Can you move? Do you want to? Why would an employer want to hire you? What is your self-perception? What do you know and believe about yourself? What are your strengths? Weaknesses? And so on, and so on, and so on....

If you don't know who you are, you will be hard-pressed to figure out what type of career you seek, and you will have an even harder time deciding what value you offer to potential employers.

Without this understanding you won't be clear on the "start point" on your transition journey.

EXAMPLE

Anyone that's ever done a land navigation course knows that if you aren't sure of your starting grid, your course is going to be a challenge...shoot an azimuth from the wrong spot and you're likely to land in yet another wrong spot...same for transition.

This is YOUR transition. You are the one who has to make the decisions (with appropriate coordination with relevant family, etc.). You are the one who has to present yourself to employers. It only makes sense to start with you!

STORY

"Zero Dark Thirty," a 2012 American thriller film directed by Kathryn Bigelow and written by Mark Boal, focused on the story around the take down of Osama bin Laden.

> *One of the final scenes shows the heroine character boarding an empty cargo aircraft, seemingly soon after mission complete. She looks a bit dazed by the recent chain of events — events that appear to place a capstone on an entire career's work.*
>
> *Upon boarding, a flight crew member says she can sit anywhere she'd like since there is no cargo and she is the only passenger. He then comments something to the effect, "You must be very important to have this aircraft all to yourself." This simple comment highlights that career transition can be a lonely time.*
>
> *He then asks the magic question, "Where do you want to go?" She looked thoroughly lost and had no words in reply.*
>
> *As I watched this scene it struck me that this is THE question for people in career transition.*

Military or not, life-long career or just starting out, transitioning by your choice or others', this question is critical to what happens next, how you approach your transition, and, ultimately, where you land.

Many people simply don't think about this question, its answer, or its impact on their future.

Oftentimes people focus on the technical, tactical stuff (resume, social media presence, etc.), which is all important, but they fail to define "where they want to go."

Take the time. Make the effort. Invest in yourself. You'll be glad you did.

Purpose has long been a hot topic in military veteran career transition.

Veterans have a high sense of purpose.

Lack of purpose (perceived or real) is often a major challenge to career transition and satisfaction once veterans land in the workplace.

Getting clear on your purpose will focus you and help optimize your transition. It will:

★ Help you build a better network.

★ Begin to clarify how you fit and can add value to a new, dynamic work world.

★ Lead to higher-level results (e.g., landing a better job/ career sooner, greater success and satisfaction on the job once landed, etc.).

★ Broaden your view by considering the entire career playing field, not just a narrow environment with which you are familiar.

★ Help you clarify your "elevator pitch" — your answer to the dreaded "Tell me about yourself" question. This clarity is critical beyond the simple act of responding to specific questions. It helps others understand who you are and where you are going, and thus enables them to better help you along the way.

★ Help you to prioritize your efforts. The unfamiliar world of career transition is full of new, unknown challenges and opportunities. Clarifying your purpose gives you a centering point upon which to focus and select high-payoff actions to optimize your search.

As with so many things in life, this purpose work is only valuable if translated to action. When considering your purpose look "inward and back," and "outward and forward."

★ Looking inward and back helps to identify where you've been, how you got here, and what makes you unique. It helps to clarify "who you are and what you are bringing to the party."

★ Looking outward and forward gives you a better view of the terrain you are about to enter and the various challenges and opportunities it holds.

Optimizing your transition is hard work. It takes dedication, effort, reliance on your existing capabilities, and a willingness to push yourself beyond what you've known for years. It takes humility and vulnerability to open yourself to new people, new perspectives, new challenges, new opportunities.

Invest in yourself. Take the time and the effort to define your purpose. Find a partner, coach, or other who will help. The upside of this investment will be well worth it!

2. Define "Success." What does "good" look like for you relative to your transition and future career, professionally and personally? This differs from the prior step in that we are now identifying how you will know when you "win." Are you scoring touchdowns (where the most points win), or are you playing golf (where the lowest score wins)? Understanding how you define and measure success helps you clarify your target job/career, build your transition strategy/plan, and consider opportunities when they arise.

Having worked through these two important steps, it's a good time to check on what you want to do. While there are many variables that go into this, I'll suggest a great framework to start with is to consider three things:

★ What am I best at?

★ What am I passionate about?

★ What meets the pragmatic realities of my situation (family, finances, timing, etc.)?

Find the intersection of these three, and you have a pretty good idea of careers/jobs that might be a great fit for you. The answers may not come right away. This is an iterative process. Repetition, review, and revisiting your prior thoughts all add clarity over time. The sooner you start, the sooner you are likely to come to a top-notch decision.

3. Learn everything you can about your transition environment — the work world you are about to enter. This is the "intelligence preparation of the battlefield" wherein you thoughtfully consider the world you are facing from every possible dimension. From high-level, macro topics (geopolitics, industry trends, societal issues, etc.) to the particulars of your network, search tools, preferred companies and jobs, and others, this work is critical to ensuring you understand the world you are facing and are properly preparing for success in it.

4. Identify and prioritize the gaps between you, your capabilities, how you define success, and the realities of your transition environment. You will have much to do and wasting time and energy on non-value-adding activity is not good.

5. Close the gaps — This is the action planning step. In this step you build plans to close select gaps and refine your search strategy.

6. Execute your plan. Check progress. Conduct after-action-reviews. Adjust as needed. Keep driving forward.

73
"Self-perception" — is it helping or hurting you?

What do you see when you think of yourself? A service member? Or civilian employee? At first, it is normal to see yourself as a service member. After all, you've spent the preceding years or decades as a service member in a very specific culture with an amazingly robust training and development capability.

All this said, it is important that you begin to evolve that identity and begin to see yourself as the person best capable to do the work you plan on doing.

Employers are not hiring service members or veterans. They are hiring people they believe best qualified to do the work they need done and who they believe will best fit and add value to their culture.

Does this mean you have to hide your military service? To push away all the great training, development, and experience you've garnered over the years? Certainly NOT!

Your military service and experience have prepared you with great attributes that can bring real value to employers. The key here is to adjust your perspective, to be respectful of your past, leverage all the positives, and see yourself in a new light — one that makes you shine in the eyes of potential employers as the best fit.

This is important because if you don't see yourself through this lens and believe in yourself as the best possible person to answer the employer's needs, you make it nearly impossible for the employer to see you as the top candidate to fill their needs (after all, you are the employer's biggest window into you and your potential to fill their open job).

STORY

A colleague of mine told me of a veteran she hired several months before for an industrial sales role. He was performing quite well, hitting his sales targets, administering sales properly, and getting along reasonably well with his customers. The challenge was with his internal team. They all recognized his sales skills and success. Their concern was that his frame of reference was all military. His conversations, stories, and examples were all military. None of his teammates were veterans, and this was not a defense contractor. His perspective was so foreign that the team began listening to him less and less. They stopped sharing information with him as they once did. They were simply sick of the "war stories." The story ended well. My colleague addressed the issue with the veteran, who took the feedback and made improvements. The relationship with his team eventually improved but valuable time was lost.

Similarly, it is important to gain awareness of how you present yourself and what employers see when they think of *you.* Do they see you as a forward-looking, value-adding team member? Or do they see you as a rearward-looking veteran with an unrelenting hold on the culture you are leaving? If the latter, you are at risk of fulfilling many of the employer's preconceived notions and biases, and you are at risk for not being the candidate of choice.

Make this awareness of your self-perception and others' perception of you a part of your transition preparation. Seek network connections who are able to give you objective feedback. Adjust as needed.

74

Aspiration is one thing. Action is another.
You'll need both for success.

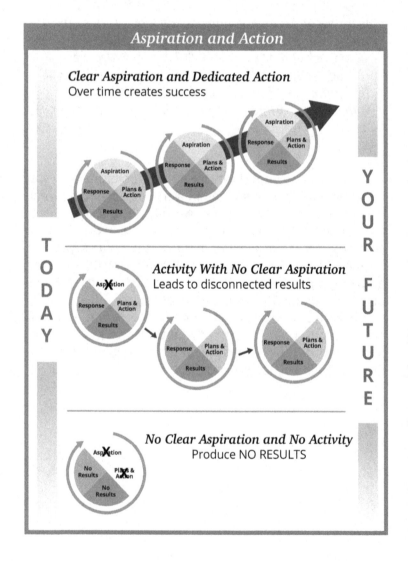

75

The "framework" of your past career is gone. You must create your own.

One day I was discussing career transition with a soon-to-be veteran. Our chat veered toward fear of the unknown and how hard it might be to stay focused in this foreign situation where opportunities are seemingly endless, clear paths to success are rarely obvious, and the framework of the military organization, structure, and culture is gone.

Being part of an organization (especially one as structured and disciplined as the military) brings with it some tremendous (although often unrecognized/underappreciated) benefits. Among these are purpose, structure, context, momentum, and similar factors that provide environmental inertia to keep you on track and moving forward.

These factors are part of the framework within which you bring to bear your experience, skills, abilities, etc. to make things happen. One might suggest they are like bumpers in bumper bowling, nudging you back into the lane when you are heading for the gutters.

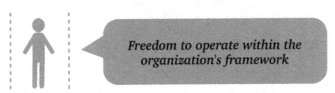

Freedom to operate within the organization's framework

When you separate from the organization, the framework is gone. No longer can you count on the organization's framework. You are on your own to make your way forward.

So, how do you create your own framework? I'll suggest you must change your perspective. Look no longer for those external boundaries and motivators to keep you moving and on track. Rather, look internally to create your own framework.

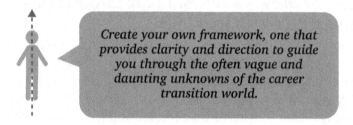

Create your own framework, one that provides clarity and direction to guide you through the often vague and daunting unknowns of the career transition world.

This is an amazing opportunity to figure out who you are and what you really bring to the party.

★ What are your guiding principles? Your core values?

★ What are your preferences? Your non-negotiables?

★ What do you want? What do you need?

★ What are your constraints and obligations?

★ What motivates you? What matters to you?

★ What are you best at?

★ How can you make money?

★ What are you passionate about?

★ How do you define success?

Answering these questions may be hard. This may be the first time in your life you've had such an open field in front of you. It may be scary.

You may believe you don't have answers, but you do. You make decisions every day that influence or are influenced by these questions.

Doing this work enables you to change your perspective. You no longer need an organizational framework to keep you on track and moving forward. You now have an azimuth, a direction, and some clarity about what you're doing, where you're going, and how you're going about it. Your answers may change over time. That's OK. Doing this work will pay huge dividends.

Leveraging this work along with effective networking, diligent overall effort, and a confident, positive demeanor will optimize your transition experience.

76

Leverage your experience and tools to optimize transition success.

Your military career, training, and experience provide you with a fantastic launch point for a civilian career. You learned many valuable tools, processes, and techniques that can help you through transition. Some are technical "hard" skills. Some are "soft" skills. All are potentially relevant. They are tools in your toolbox that can be especially effective when facing uncertain/unfamiliar situations — like career transition.

77

Leading versus managing your transition.

Are you leading your transition or managing it?

Are you doing the right things or are you doing things right?

Are you busy or are you adding value?

How do you know?

Properly leading and managing your career transition can be a challenge. Each career transition comes with its own circumstances, opportunities, and challenges. Everyone in career transition approaches it in their own unique way.

That said, there are some common keys to transition success:

★ Define your target and focus on the mission.

★ Maintain situational awareness and minimize distractions.

★ Manage the administrivia in a way that works for you (but be wary of over-managing them).

★ Build in a way that keeps your transition on track (I suggest a "Daily Check In").
  ★ What is my overall mission?
  ★ Current status?
  ★ Right things to do today? How do I do them right?

★ Be aware that there are different career transition phases; plan properly for each.
  ★ Pre-transition.
  ★ Transition (exit, search, selection).
  ★ Start and assimilation.
  ★ Thriving.

★ Be mindful of the phrase "you go where your thoughts are." Think of success, growth, positive potential, victory, and you will go there. Think fixed, stagnant, negative, defeating thoughts and there you will land.

★ Leverage routine as much as possible to reinforce at least some bits of consistency.

As with so many things in life, *balance* is key for career transition. Keeping balance top-of-mind throughout your transition is a great way to ensure you are leading and managing it effectively. Examples of things to balance:

★ Past/present.

★ Today/tomorrow.

★ Passion/pragmatism.

★ Work/life.

★ Current job requirements/transition needs.

★ Confidence/competence.

★ Employer requirements (asks)/your capabilities and expectations (answers).

78

Keep your eye on the ball...daily kibbles and bits can distract you.

Sometimes in new, unfamiliar situations identifying and staying focused on the real goal is tough. It is no different in career transition. At first you may have no idea what your goal is or how to achieve it.

You must be wary of not getting too distracted by things that don't matter. Keep situational awareness of all the moving bits and develop your ability to understand their impact on your goal. You will get good at this with practice.

A great example of this is chasing your number of "connections" on LinkedIn. In and of itself, this metric is a bit useless. Yes, career transition success is impacted by growing a network but the sheer numbers are not the key. The key is to connect with people who are relevant to your mission and can help you achieve your goal.

Check to see that if what is distracting you is adding value or not. If so, great! New opportunities and perspectives are wonderful. If not, re-focus back on your mission. Seek and maintain balance. You'll be glad you did!

79
You will get tons of advice.

> *"About some things it is not possible to make a universal statement which shall be correct." — Aristotle*

My guess is that Aristotle didn't have career transition in mind, but this certainly applies.

As you travel your transition journey you will hear vast amounts of input, opinions, thoughts, ideas, and best practices.

Some will come from folks with great experience on both sides of the transition desk.

Some will come from folks with strong opinions but little experience.

Some will come from folks with particular agendas.

Much of it will be similar with minor variations.

Some will be dramatically different.

Take it all in. Consider it all. Use what best resonates with you. Keep the rest as information that rounds out your perspective and/or tools that you may find useful later.

80
Transition moves at the speed of you.

Optempo — the speed/pace at which the situation and people move — is a significant concern that, if misaligned, can derail your career transition and longer-term employment success.

Every person, organization, circumstance and job have a particular optempo.

★ Chess is played at a certain speed — as is hockey.

★ Police on long-term surveillance move at a different optempo than those in hot pursuit.

★ Workplace optempo for a research scientist is clearly different than for an emergency responder.

Do you know your personal optempo? Do you tend to be a fast-paced multitasker? Or are you slower paced and methodical? Where do you do your best work? Where are you most comfortable?

What about the general optempo of the industry or career field that interests you? Is it a fast-paced, dynamic environment? Or is it perhaps more stable, predictable, and slow to change?

Beyond this, how does your optempo compare to that of the particular organization/company you are seeking to join? Is this a fast-moving, growing company with high aspirations and high energy? Or is it a more mature company that is established in its ways, perhaps a bit comfortable and happy to ride the wave of its previous success?

And finally, what about the optempo of the specific job for which you might apply?

★ Fast or slow, dynamic or static, multitasking or focused — in and of themselves these are neither right nor wrong.

★ The challenge comes when your optempo doesn't align with the optempo of the others.

★ If misaligned, you will find yourself either ahead of or behind the power curve, restrained by the bridle of others' slower pace, or stung by the drivers' crop as they push you to move faster.

As you consider your career transition, do your homework. Consider your optempo. Look at the industries, companies, and jobs that best align. Make informed choices, and take actions that will optimize your success.

81

Take a break before you break.

Most automobile owners know that to properly care for your car, you must periodically stop, shut it down, check and service critical systems and components, change the oil, filters, etc., and add more fuel. You must give it a break.

Failing to do so causes it to (at best) simply run out of gas or (at worst) break down.

In either case, your journey is interrupted ... by a thoroughly avoidable circumstance.

Think of high-stakes automobile races ... they all have pit stops.

For many people, career transition is a high-stress, foreign environment. It requires action and engagement. Know your "redline" and when to exceed it — sometimes you need to hit overdrive to keep up with opportunities. Sometimes you need to get off the gas, get off the track, and take a pit stop.

Most people in career transition are new to it. They crank up their level of focus, work, attention, and activity. They see the unknown landscape ahead and do everything possible to do the transition work while learning on-the-fly what that work really is.

Many folks approach transition with great resilience by taking action to influence the situation and always doing more to make things happen.

Certainly, this is critical to creating success, but similar to our cars, we all need a break.

The question is — are you ready, willing, and able to do so?

Taking a break seems counterintuitive for many. After all, there is work to be done!

So, how do we get ready, willing, and able to take the breaks? I'll suggest the following:

★ **Recognize that transition is an endurance race.** Your course, tools, equipment, and crew may not be perfectly clear at the start, but one thing is certain — this race will likely last longer than anyone would prefer.

★ **Acknowledge that you will be learning as you go — which takes time, effort, energy and attention.** Your hard work and work plan will evolve over time. Your efficiency and effectiveness will improve as you go. Be OK with making mistakes as you learn, then learn from your mistakes.

★ **Be willing to take care of yourself along the journey.** Value yourself highly enough to invest in your own recovery. Know that you must occasionally "refit" so you can fight another day.

★ **Plan your efforts so as to be able to take breaks.** Career transition is a fluid, uncertain environment that is unsettling for many. Building in planned breaks and sticking to them diligently provides some certainty that can be very helpful to your long-term success.

★ **Take mini-breaks.** Get away from the grind for a few minutes every day — physically, mentally, emotionally. Let things go at night. Sleep. Let not the concerns of the day invade your night.

★ **Be confident enough to take breaks.** The transition situation may be tougher than you expected but you have done tough things well. Stop. Recharge. Return to the fight.

STORY

In my 2017 TEDx Toledo talk "Investing in the Middle," I speak about this. Many times, people and organizations approach work (in this case transition) by trying to "sprint an entire marathon" — giving every bit of energy with every step to move as quickly as possible for as long as possible. We all know this is impossible. I suggest career transition is more of a road march in which one carries a heavy load over a challenging and perhaps unknown course. It is hard work. It does not always move quickly. But well-planned road marches always build in breaks ... breaks to check your feet, change your socks, and adjust your load (and experienced folks also verify their course and direction). Conduct your transition like a road march — build in the breaks.

82

"Calm urgency" — balance progress and patience to optimize transition.

Transition can get frustrating, hectic, crazy, and unnerving. It can wear you down if you let it.

Don't let it. Establish a sense of "calm urgency" to keep your cool AND move forward with appropriate speed, priority, clarity, and purpose.

There are times when you must seize the moment, react swiftly, and move fast, but that isn't every moment of every day.

Think of the great leaders in your life. Likely one of the characteristics you most valued from them was their ability to stay calm under pressure while continuing to drive forward. They maintained a sense of urgency.

When your transition gets stressful, focus on calm urgency. Take a breath and stay calm — look realistically at the situation, its nature, magnitude, and impact; far too often we make things worse than they are or ever could be.

83

Take stock of all that is good, safe, and unchanging through your transition.

Career transition can be a challenging, uncomfortable time. So much to do. So much is new.

It can get to you if you let it. Don't let it. When it happens to you, take a pause to look for and appreciate all that is good, all that is safe, all that is unchanging.

84

Transition is a lonely time. Stay connected with people. Remember your family — they are going through this too.

'Nuff said ...

85

Realize that work and life are less a balance and more a blend...you get to decide how much of each is right for you.

Balance implies opposites — as in two kids at opposite ends of the playground teeter-totter. I'll suggest that career transition (and life) is best when considered a blend rather than a balance.

Work is important, life is important — but they are simply two ingredients in the same recipe. We each have different tastes and preferences. Some prefer stew, some chili, others prefer cake. No matter the meal, each takes the right blend of unique ingredients to taste great — and that right blend varies from person to person.

Decide what you're hungry for, research the recipe, then blend ingredients to your liking!

86

Keep your eyes and ears open to new perspectives and possibilities.

While focus is critical in career transition, one must also be open to new perspectives and possibilities that may come out of nowhere!

Some of them will be garbage. Some will be interesting but hard to understand. Some will be awesome!

In the beginning, you may not be sure what to do with these new perspectives and possibilities. How do I assess them? What do I do with them? How do I decide which ones to chase and which ones to toss?

Be open to receiving them all. You will develop your ability to vet them for further action along the way!

STORY

Sun Tzu and Career Transition — Being open to new perspectives includes considering the value of age-old lessons from a different context. As amazing as it may sound, even Sun Tzu, the legendary thought-leader on all matters related to military arts and science, has relevant thoughts!

Sun Tzu and...Career Transition?

Sun Tzu	Transition
"In the midst of chaos, there is also opportunity."	Transition is foreign and chaotic. Keep your eyes and ears open for unexpected opportunity.
"The general who wins the battle makes many calculations in his temple before the battle is fought. The general who loses makes but few calculations beforehand."	Start preparing for transition early.
"Strategy without tactics is the slowest route to victory. Tactics without strategy is the noise before defeat."	What are you here to do? What are the right things to do today? How do you do them right?
"Victory comes from finding opportunities in problems."	Don't get discouraged. Work through the problems. Find the way forward.
"The good fighters of old first put themselves beyond the possibility of defeat, and then waited for an opportunity of defeating the enemy."	A large part of transition success is believing in yourself.
"Opportunities multiply as they are seized."	Once seized, opportunity can create transition momentum!
"The skillful employer of men will employ the wise man, the brave man, the covetous man, and the stupid man."	Employers always seek top talent!
"You have to believe in yourself."	Confidence drives action; action begets success; success begets success.
"Sweat more during peace; bleed less during war."	Train, learn, and prepare — before you transition.

(continued)

Sun Tzu and...Career Transition?

Sun Tzu	Transition
"Knowing the enemy enables you to take the offensive, knowing yourself enables you to stand on the defensive."	Understand the employer's "ASKS" and your "ANSWERS" to each. Then go present yourself as the best candidate to fill their need.
"Using order to deal with the disorderly, using calm to deal with the clamorous, is mastering the heart."	"Calm Urgency" — the key to traveling the confusing, frustrating, unfamiliar transition journey well.
"Move not unless you see an advantage; use not your troops unless there is something to be gained; fight not unless the position is critical."	Are you busy or adding value? What are you asking your network to do for you? Are you chasing "unicorns" or are you taking meaningful steps to your goal?
"All wars are won or lost before they are ever fought."	Plan and prepare well, long before transition.
"Rewards for good service should not be deferred a single day."	Transition has its good days and bad. Find a win, no matter how small, every day. Allow yourself to enjoy it.
"Ponder and deliberate before you make a move."	"Fire, Aim, Ready". It didn't work for Sun Tzu and it won't work for your transition either.
"When your opponent gives you an opening, be swift as a hare."	When a job opportunity appears, get on it! Your competition surely is.
"Concentrate your energy and hoard your strength."	In transition it is tempting to "chase shiny things." Don't waste your energy. Define your target and put all efforts towards it.
"If ignorant both of your enemy and yourself, you are certain to be in peril."	Two basic keys to transition success are to 1) Know "Who You Are and What You Bring to the Party" and 2) your "transition environment."

87

Informational interviews *are important.*

Informational interviews are simply conversations with people who have knowledge/experience in a job, company, industry, or other area you want to learn more about. Typically, initial ones are brief (15 to 20 minutes). Subsequent ones may be longer.

They are amazingly effective on a number of levels.

★ Connecting with someone new.

★ Learning new information that you specifically seek.

★ Opening doors to new ideas and possibly new opportunities.

When conducting an informational interview:

★ Have a purpose.

★ Respect the other party's time.

★ Be professional.

★ Ask, listen, and converse well.

★ Thank the other party and ask for any additional thoughts, guidance, or contacts they can recommend.

88

Learn the language of your desired career field by meeting people, reading job descriptions, etc.

No matter how much someone may want to help you (and most do), things get exponentially harder when you are speaking a different language.

In career transition, it is your job to learn the language the employers speak — not their job to learn Mil-speak or Veteran-ese. After all, you are entering their world; they are not joining the military.

Get started on this early. Begin reading about the jobs, careers, companies, and industries that interest you. Connect with people working in those areas. Find job descriptions/job postings for the jobs that you seek. Read them. Pay attention to the language. If you don't know or understand it, learn!

It's your job to tell your story in a way that lands well on the employer's ear. Do your homework early. You can't "cram for the exam" when it comes to language.

89

Don't shy away from rejection.

Rejection is a pervasive part of career transition. It can hurt if you let it.

When it happens to you (and it will — more than once) take the sting and use it to improve your plan, actions, approach, and overall strategy. As a military veteran, one of the greatest capabilities you likely have is agility. When you are rejected, lean on your agility to find new ways through, over, around, or under the obstacles that contributed to the rejection.

90

The transition journey is not a straight, flat path. Be resilient.

The path to your goal may need more interim steps than you thought. Hurdles will pop up. Potholes will appear.

You may not get to your goal exactly the way or in the time you first thought, but you will get there. Take careful stock of your situation. If you're wrong, adjust. If you're right, stand your ground and overcome the challenge. Resilience and positive perspective make all the difference!

91

When an amazing opportunity arises, seize the moment. Grab it and run with it; vet it fast and hard; know your decision criteria and your worth.

As you transition, you may run across what appear to be amazing opportunities. These "shiny things" may/may not really be awesome. They may/may not be open for long, so you need to have a plan for how you deal with these targets of opportunity.

★ Understand what your real goal is. Be as clear as possible about your critical success criteria.

★ Move quickly to get as much information as possible about the opportunity. Check with your network to see if anyone has insights and/or connections that may help.

★ Be open to these opportunities, but be purposeful in your approach. Cynicism won't help, but a healthy dose of thoughtful consideration is certainly in order.

92

Remember — people are watching. To see you win. To see you fail. To see how you're doing it.

Career transition may feel lonely but you are rarely alone. Your family, members of the tribe you are leaving, new network connections, recruiters, employers, and a host of others are all around you and, in varying ways, are sharing the journey with you.

Some are rooting for you. Some are watching what you do and how you do it so that they might learn from your successes and failures and be better prepared for their own transition. Some are watching to see if/how you and your capabilities might fit and add value to their teams.

Regardless the reason, you are not alone. Others will have eyes on you.

93

Your integrity may be tested. Know who you are and what you stand for because in the end all we have is our honor.

Years ago, when being considered for my first company command, I was required to prepare and present my "Philosophy of Command" to the brigade commander who would decide which young captain should fill the command job.

Others in my position typically prepared three-ring binders of leadership materials that resonated with them. I took a different path. I figured that when I'd need to lean on these values most, I likely wouldn't have a three-ring binder with me. So, I decided to get as much clarity as possible and put my thoughts on a 3 × 5-inch card which I would be able to carry with me anywhere.

The six words I put on the card are listed below with their core meaning to me.

Initiative — Get up and do something. Few people are successful lounging on the couch.

Integrity — Whatever you do, do it with complete integrity, because in the end all we really have is our honor.

Focus — Be focused on the matter at hand. Be present for the situation and the people around you.

Foresight — Realize that today's actions will impact tomorrow.

Commitment — Whatever you do, give it 150% — no one ever realized their potential by going halfway.

Common Sense — If something doesn't seem to make sense, there's a real possibility that it doesn't make sense.

While this unconventional approach created an *interesting* (if not easy) conversation with the brigade commander, it provided me clarity that continues to serve me to this very day.

94

People along the way may "promise you the ride" (make connections, give you exposure to opportunities, etc.) but no one will promise you the "win." You have to earn that.

As you travel your transition journey, you will meet a vast array of people. Most want to help. Some are more able to help than others. Some will over-promise and under-deliver. Some will try to exploit you to advance whatever their cause might be.

Be open. Pay attention. Trust but verify. Be mindful that no matter what others offer and/or deliver, transition is your work to do.

95

Your transition will bog down. It's your job to kick start it.

Hard as it may be, remember that career transition, at its root, is just a very big decision exercise. You'll likely have more decisions to make with less knowledge/experience, and fewer allies than ever before.

When it gets tough, remember to:

★ First identify the problem(s).

★ Leverage your decision-making expertise.

★ Assess the situation.

★ Define root cause(s).

★ Develop courses of action.

★ Consult with trusted others, then decide, execute, and iterate.

Key areas where transitions can bog down:

★ *Your target —*

    ★ *Job/Career* — The demand for your target job/career may be declining (e.g., there are very few buggy whip manufacturing jobs since the automobile hit the market).

    ★ *Market/Industry* — Similar to jobs/careers, markets and industries shift. For example, movie theaters have been negatively impacted by the availability of video streaming, and UBER and similar ride-share businesses have hurt car rental companies. Multiple other industries have also been impacted by the 2020 global pandemic.

★ *You* — As your transition evolves, you may find that it impacts your attitude, wearing you down to a less-than-positive place. You may find that your aspiration may not match your experience and qualifications. Stay positive.

  ★ *Your behavior/activity* — You may have to change how you go about your transition. Carefully assess how you are searching, how you are networking, how you are building your brand, and how you are managing your transition to discover opportunities for improvement.

  ★ *Your surroundings/geography* — Sometimes your surroundings can bog you down. Consider if/how the people in your network, where you hang out, your current location versus your target location are impacting your transition progress. If you want to catch tuna, you don't fish in the Great Lakes.

96

When you are approaching the finish line and it's clear you're going to win, remember your teammates. Do the right thing to bring them across with you.

At some point all of your hard work is going to pay off. You will land.

When you do, you'll have new things to learn, new people to meet, new tasks, new schedules, and so on. Attend to them. As flight attendants always remind us, "Put your oxygen mask on first before helping others."

Remember, however, you didn't make this journey alone. Many people helped you along the way. They are part of your network — not just for your most recent transition, but for life. Thank them. Help them as they may need. Be there for them as they were there for you, so they can achieve success as they define it.

97

Have some fun along the way.

A good friend who grew up surfing offered this perspective on career transition.

> *My goal was always to ride the perfect wave.*
>
> *First, I learned how to surf.*
>
> *Then I learned how to read the waves, how to position myself in the water, and so on.*
>
> *I surfed every chance I got (much to the chagrin of my parents and teachers).*
>
> *Waves came and went.*
>
> *Some I rode. I passed on many.*
>
> *I learned. I got strong. I got better. I love my life.*

The point to all this?

> A detailed plan isn't always critical for success.
>
> Have a goal.
>
> Do the work.
>
> Have some fun along the way.

NETWORKING

98

If you want to do NEWwork, your NOWwork is to NETwork.

I'm often asked, "What's the best thing to do to build a successful career?" "How do I make sure I advance my career?" and similar questions.

There is no magic bullet. No single answer. There are, however, common threads that if, all done well, may add up to a great, successful career.

First, let's get clear on "success." It means something different to everyone. There is no one grand definition or path to it. Thus, Step 1 in building a successful career is to get clear on how you define it.

★ A high-level title (think CEO)?

★ Being a master craftsman working in your own individual shop, earning enough money to keep you and your family safe and secure?

★ Being a reliable member of a medical staff at a center serving remote, underserved people?

★ Leading the IT function for a complex, global, commercial firm?

★ Other?

This done, action and attention are required in three key areas:

"NOWwork"

Always do a great job at the job you are in. This is the baseline for everything else. It provides experience. It builds your reputation and your credibility. Being known as the one who "gets it done" is critical.

Equally critical is the manner in which you do the work. Being a high-producing jerk is a no-go. People will not want to work with you — no matter how many goals you knock down. If you can't get along with people (peers, managers, employees, customers, suppliers, etc.) your success will be limited.

Continually improve. Learn more about the breadth and depth of your job. Practice, practice, practice. Learn from your mistakes. Listen to constructive criticism. Perform your own after-action reviews. Apply what you learn so that you can do better tomorrow than you did today.

"NEWwork"

Career advancement almost always means learning and applying something new. Larger, more senior roles generally include broader, deeper, more complex scopes of responsibility. If you aspire to these, it's important that you understand these duties and take action to become familiar with and skilled at these.

Even if your aspiration is more individual and not tied to the typical upward progression definition of career success, NEWwork is important. Tools, technologies, techniques, markets, and so many other factors evolve over time. Keeping up with these advancements is deeply valuable to optimizing your long-term success.

"NETwork"

No one is an island. No matter the career/job, we all impact and are impacted by others. Even the most reclusive-sounding careers have some interaction with others, perhaps only for acquiring supplies or only with customers who buy our goods. BUT we all have and need some degree of NETwork.

Without a NETwork, great NOWwork and NEWwork go unnoticed. The good word of your good works goes unshared. You get caught up in a loop of perpetual effort with little/no career progress.

Networking can be challenging for people. Some just don't like it. Some aren't sure how to do it. Some are so focused on the NOW and NEW that they just don't focus on it. Regardless of reason, if networking is not addressed, career success will not be optimized.

There are myriad great resources available at the click of your mouse to help address all these areas.

The bottom line is that all three are important and career success is optimized when you attend to and take action for each.

STORY

One day a gentleman was hungry for stew. He knew nothing about stew other than he remembered how he loved the stew his grandma made when he was a kid. He could have run to the store to buy a can of "Dinty Moore" but that isn't what he wanted. So, he decided he'd learn how to make Grandma's stew. He researched what it takes to make the stew. He didn't have the recipe, so he connected with siblings, cousins, and other family members. None of them had Grandma's recipe but they offered their opinions about how they thought she made it. He tried several. None were right. He continued seeking people who might know until he came upon a neighborhood friend of his grandma's. She had the recipe! Ingredients, proportions, pot type, time, temperature, all of it! He used that recipe to make the stew. It didn't taste right. Considering what might have gone wrong, he did some more homework and talked with a few folks. He concluded that the vegetables he used were not ripe. How was he sup-

posed to know that? So, he learned all about the proper ripeness of vegetables to use in stew. He tried again. It was better! He continued trying until finally the soup was just like Grandma's.

Yes, he could have skipped the hard stuff and bought a can of Dinty Moore. He could have stopped anywhere along the line, settling for something that was close. But he knew what he wanted and those were not it! Do the work transition requires. Network with people. The end result will be worth it!

99
Networking is a conversation with a purpose.

It is more than idle chit-chat. It is more than social small talk. It is about connecting with people to establish a relationship that is beneficial to you and the other party... toward achieving some purpose.

100
If you want employers to know you, network with them.

Some folks avoid networking. Some are shy or introverted. Some consider networking as a form of manipulation. Others simply don't know "how" to do it. Reasons vary for everyone but common themes include:

★ Getting "busy doing today." Focusing on delivering the dailies in the world with which they are so familiar.

★ Lack of awareness of just how important it is to connect with people who are in the world you seek to join (and/or how to do it).

★ Ego/overconfidence — "I don't need to network! I'm highly educated, experienced, and have awesome capability; any employer would be lucky to have me on their team."

★ Fear — of the unknown, of appearing vulnerable, of "leaving the nest," etc.

This all is quite unfortunate because the harsh reality is that networking is the Number 1 means of landing a job. Some studies show that over 80% of jobs are landed because of networking. In fact, most often it is the second- or third-tier network connections that are key to finding and landing a job. This means someone you know knows someone who knows of an opportunity. Yep. Networks are critical.

Be bold. Take the initiative to get over your fears, over yourself, over your focus on today, or any other hurdles.

STORY

When I first transitioned out of the military, I avoided networking like the plague. I didn't know what to do or how to do it. I figured my achievements in the military would be so appealing that there would be little need to network.

I was wrong. Without networking, no one even knew of my achievements, experience, or expertise. I wasn't telling my story and neither was anyone else!

The lightbulb eventually went on. I got over myself and began networking. I was clumsy at first. I was embar-

> *rassed. But I pressed on. I kept working at it. I got better.*
> *Word of my capabilities began to get around. A few peo-*
> *ple called back, sharing opportunities they thought might*
> *be a good fit for me.*
>
> *It was a rocky start but one connection led to two, two*
> *to four, and so on — all of which were important steps on*
> *my success journey.*

101

Hooking up a brother/sister— the essence of NETWORKING!

We all know this phrase. We've heard it throughout our military careers. You ask a friend/colleague to help you get something you need.

It requires action on your part to make the Ask.
It requires a response from the other party.

It works where you have a common connection.
It works best where you have a relationship.

The process works the same in transition! It may be foreign territory, but there are people along the way who have what you need.

- ★ Contact them.

- ★ Connect with them.

- ★ Build a relationship.

- ★ Figure out what your Ask is, then ask for the hook up.

102

Similar to SOF (Special Operations Forces) Truth 5: "Most special operations require non-SOF assistance." When in transition, you will need lots of support from folks with different experiences and expertise.

Transition is a lonely time. The work environment you've lived in throughout your prior career is gone. Many of the people with whom you associate are either remaining in that world (not yet transitioning) or moving in their own transition directions. You will have to build a new network.

Leverage your current support structure.

Connect with new people.

Build a solid team around you to accomplish your transition mission.

Build a support network by building relationships (a "...state of being connected...the way in which two or more people regard and behave toward each other...").

Reach out to people familiar and new.

- ★ Present the best possible you.
- ★ Be genuinely interested in others:
    - ★ Listen to their words.
    - ★ Offer value-adding responses.
    - ★ Help where you can.
    - ★ Display the confidence that demonstrates your value.
- ★ Demonstrate the humility to accept help where it is offered.

Note: As a great mentor of mine always said "It's better to be a 'go-giver' than a 'go-getter.' Invest in the relationships and the jobs will come."

103
Network hierarchy and growth.

What is a network? It is people with whom you've made contact/connection that may be able to help you succeed.

Think of your network as a living thing. It grows and matures based on the quantity and quality of care and attention you provide.

Networks grow according to a typical pattern:

★ First, there is some level of *awareness* of another person. Perhaps you saw their profile on LinkedIn, someone recommended them to you, you heard their name in passing, or they popped up in the news or social media. Regardless of method, somehow you became aware of this person and had some type of interest.

★ Next, there is some manner of *contact*. Perhaps you pinged them on LinkedIn. Maybe a mutual connection made an introduction. Maybe you ran into each other at a company or industry event, a social gathering, or the grocery store. The point here is that in some way contact was made.

★ Next, a *connection* may develop. This is beyond contact. Have you ever ridden a busy subway? You bump into innumerable people. That is contact. Yet there is no connection. Beyond the random act of being in the same place at the same time, there is nothing that causes you to "connect." Connecting requires action. To connect with someone, you must make an effort beyond a simple introduction, a simple greeting, a blind invite in LinkedIn, a casual passing of business cards at a meeting. Reach out. Ask how the person is doing, inquire about their work, their interests, etc. Share a bit about yourself, your work, your interests. At some point, when some level of rapport is built, let the other person know what you are looking for, what your purpose is. Be clear. Be concise. Be complete. Be respectful. Be professional.

★ *Relationships* develop as connections evolve. The familiarity and value-add become deeper and more important, and the willingness to go above and beyond for each other expands.

★ At the pinnacle of this hierarchy are *advocates.* These are people in your network who go above and beyond for you. They actively promote you and help advance your cause. Some of these may be folks you've known for a long time. Some may be close friends. Others may be less familiar to you. They may be senior to you, a peer, or junior. They may come from your same team, or from outside your team. They may be people inside your organization (or the organization you are targeting in your search), or they may be outside that organization but with some connection or leverage point to it. Regardless of where advocates come from, the key is that they have the interest, credibility, and ability to influence people on your behalf.

Your network includes people in all these phases.

STORY

An advocate in one circumstance may not be an advocate in another. For example, I'm reminded of a gentleman (let's call him Fred) who reached out to a connection he hadn't seen in over 20 years (John), when they worked together. Life and career opportunities took them down different paths. Both had been quite successful but they were both very busy over the years and simply hadn't stayed in regular contact. Fred was changing careers. He reached out to John. They rekindled the connection and through that reconnection John introduced Fred to several of his connections. He actively advocated with these connections to give Fred an ear, to hear what he had to say, and to afford him an opportunity if there was a need he could fill. Fred took action — he called John. John took action — he advocated for Fred. And because of this Fred landed a job. Not with one of John's direct contacts, but with someone they knew who knew of an opportunity. Networking in action.

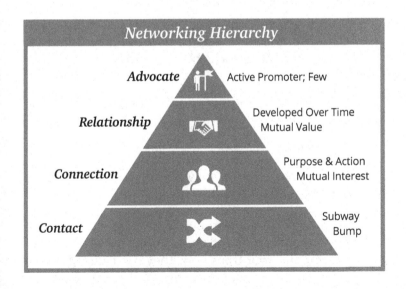

104

There are different roles network members can play.

Some people in your network are close, long-term, dear friends. Some are colleagues you know from work, school, or other social groups. Some are family. Some are present in your daily life, while others you may not have seen or chatted with in decades. Some have common experience and perspective. Some are dramatically different, offering a great depth and breadth of diverse perspective.

People in your network play different roles.

- ★ Some are the *sounding boards* — a set of ears with which you can share your thoughts.

- ★ Others are the *blind faithful* who offer a mirror/echo chamber of your every thought.

- ★ Still others are *naysayers and devil's advocates* who provide critical insight and perspective that may help you sharpen your focus or bring pragmatism to your passion.

- ★ Some are *technical experts* who provide knowledge in areas with which you may not be so familiar.

- ★ Some are *sage purveyors of wisdom.*

- ★ Others are *fresh eyes,* new players with bright, eager outlooks and insight.

The common thread through them all is that they are all potential connectors, and they all bring some manner of value to you and your transition. They can connect you to people, organizations, opportunities, and so on. And this...

the connections...is above all the critical piece to success in transition.

105

Know your go-to people. Lean on them. Listen to their counsel.

No one goes to the doctor to have their furnace repaired. Similar here.

Remember that networking is a conversation with a purpose. Be mindful of who might be your best counsel for what topics.

106

How do I network?

There are many opportunities to network. Some are dedicated events (live or virtual) specifically set up to connect people. Some are informal windows of opportunity that arise as you go about your daily life and routine.

Being ready to seize networking opportunities and make the most of them isn't hard — if you know some basics and can get over the natural fear many people have about meeting new people.

Some people are concerned that networking is simply manipulation. While I understand the possibility, I'll suggest the difference between the two is *intent*. Networking, when properly done, has a positive intent of seeking and offering value. Meeting and connecting with others to find points of interest that add value to both parties. Manipulation, on the other hand, tends to have singular and selfish intent: One party seeks to gain by exploiting another's position.

The image below highlights an effective approach to get comfortable with networking and to making the most of every opportunity.

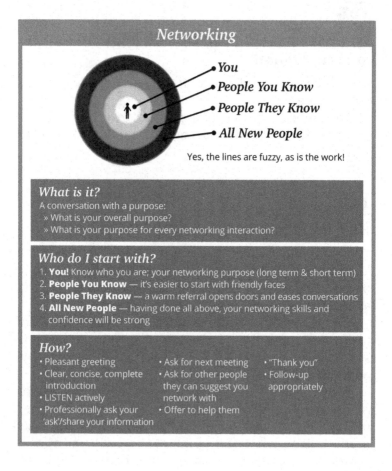

Networking

- **You**
- **People You Know**
- **People They Know**
- **All New People**

Yes, the lines are fuzzy, as is the work!

What is it?

A conversation with a purpose:
» What is your overall purpose?
» What is your purpose for every networking interaction?

Who do I start with?

1. **You!** Know who you are; your networking purpose (long term & short term)
2. **People You Know** — it's easier to start with friendly faces
3. **People They Know** — a warm referral opens doors and eases conversations
4. **All New People** — having done all above, your networking skills and confidence will be strong

How?

- Pleasant greeting
- Clear, concise, complete introduction
- LISTEN actively
- Professionally ask your 'ask'/share your information
- Ask for next meeting
- Ask for other people they can suggest you network with
- Offer to help them
- "Thank you"
- Follow-up appropriately

107

Most jobs are found via second- or third-tier connections.

Said a different way, someone you've never met knows someone else, who knows of an opportunity. If you don't actively network, you'll never be exposed to these opportunities.

108

The "elevator pitch" — your short commercial to grab attention.

You never get a chance to make a second first impression. How do you prepare to make a good one? Have a strong elevator pitch — a brief, clear, concise, complete statement that shares key information you want/need to share with new contacts.

A great mentor and friend of mine, Rich Spriggle, Senior Vice President of Challenger, Gray & Christmas, Inc., shared a great model of how to do this: "I Am, I Have, I'm Known For." This simple structure provides an efficient way for you to convey key information to new people.

I Am — a short, clear statement of your brand, for example, "I am an independent coach and advisor focused on optimizing talent capability for individuals and organizations."

I Have — a brief statement of the relevant qualifications, experiences, education, and/or other relevant information that exemplifies your credentials, for example, "I have 20-plus years' experience as a senior HR/talent management leader in large, complex, global companies designing and implementing strategies and solutions that achieve intended objectives."

*I'm Known Fo*r — a quick summary of your reputation for results, for example, "I'm known for creating innovative, effective business solutions, working effectively from the C-suite to the shop floor, and developing highly effective, enduring teams."

This model is also useful for resumes, your LinkedIn profile, and myriad other purposes. Once you get your base version down, you'll be able to adjust it on the fly for nearly any conversation or need.

109
W.A.I.T.

Networking is a conversation with a purpose. It requires conversing with other people, which includes both speaking and listening. I like to remind people that we have two ears and one mouth and suggest there might just be a reason for that.

When you are networking, you must be ready, willing, and able to tell your story, to make your Ask, and to effectively share what you have to say with others.

You must also be skilled at listening — listening for what is being said, how it is said, what it likely means to the speaker, and how it impacts you.

This won't happen if you don't stop using your mouth and start using your ears.

How do you do this? W.A.I.T. Ask yourself:

W — why

A — am

I — I

T — talking?

In the unfamiliar, sometimes fast-paced world of transition, where every word counts, take a moment to W.A.I.T.

Note — this can also be a great tool when interviewing!

110

Keep networking.

Networking is critical while in job transition. It doesn't stop once you land. As noted earlier, Networks are living things that require attention. Remember the people who helped you on your transition journey. Help them when they need it. Continue to develop new network members that positively contribute to success in your current role and that may be value-adding to your career in the future.

111

People want to help, but they can't help if they don't know what you seek.

Contrary to what many people think when new to transition, most folks really do want to help you succeed.

That said, if they don't know how to help you, the challenge is much tougher and they are much less likely to do so.

Help them help you.

Know what you want.

Know your purpose.

Know how to tell your story (clear, concise, complete) so they know how to best help you.

You'll be glad you did.

112

Be you. After all, that's who's going to show up at work every day.

"Authenticity" gets a lot of discussion these days, for good reason. We all are unique entities in this world and we all bring unique capabilities, talents, strengths, weaknesses, peculiarities, and other characteristics to it.

Being authentic does not, however, give you license to not adapt to the world around you.

Be yourself but know that others are going to be themselves also. Look for and adjust to the cultural and societal norms of your environment. Behave in a manner that is authentically you without running afoul of others. If your environment is so different that this is impossible, find a new one. No one needs to live with that bad mojo.

113

Recognize the "silverback gorillas" and the "ambitious chimps."

Not everyone you meet will provide the same insights, perspective, or value to your transition.

Some truly are heavy hitters who can open doors, clear the path, and make amazing things happen for you. Others might make a lot of noise and be quite endearing, but their zeal may far outweigh their impact and influence.

Any individual might be either. Their ability to add value may not be obvious.

While networking, pay attention to everyone. Don't dismiss anyone out of hand. Who knows? You might have just dissed the one who holds the keys to the kingdom!

114

Resilience and positive perspective make all the difference (nobody likes a party pooper/Debbie Downer).

Career transition can be a challenging time. It will get you down occasionally. Totally normal!

No one likes hanging around folks who are negative and beat down. Our friends may tolerate it from us. Familiar co-workers may be in the same headspace you are. BUT new contacts, potential new members of your network are turned off by negative, pessimistic, and similarly dour behavior.

All this said, when networking, you need to buck up and present the best, most positive version of yourself possible. If you simply can't do it, stay home. Work through your rough patch as best you can and get back out there fresh and smiling tomorrow!

TALENT ACQUISITION, RECRUITING, AND INTERVIEWING

Having prepared yourself and done all the right things in your transition, you will find opportunities that will lead to interviews. It's important to have a general understanding of how all this works.

Recruiting and interviewing are not a random set of activities. There is a general flow by which they usually happen. Yes, sometimes things get out of order. Sometimes people and organizations are more/less skilled, experienced, and capable of doing everything perfectly.

Let's start with a bit of perspective. Often folks in career transition are not familiar with any of this. They may underestimate the situation they face. After all, they bring great capability and experience to the job market, they want to work, and the path to success should be rather straightforward:

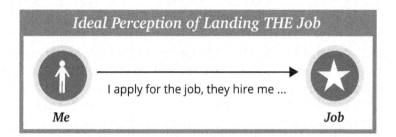

The reality of it is, however, that employers screen applicants to find the "best" fit. This screen exists to eliminate people from the process. If your resume, application, or any other document or interaction gives employers pause, is incomplete, or doesn't match the expectations for the job, you will be screened out. You'll likely never know why, and you likely will never receive feedback. You may not even get a "thanks but no thanks" message.

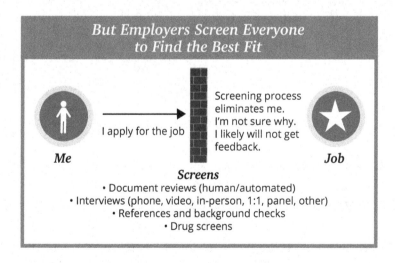

It is also important to realize that you are not the only person interested in filling an employer's open job. There are likely hundreds or even thousands of others. The sheer volume makes the competition fierce and recruiters' work-loads heavy. Much of your competition will be at least as qualified as you. Some will be far more qualified. Many will have more experience recruiting/interviewing. Recruiters must manage the volume, attend to quality, and identify the best candidates to present to hiring managers for inter-view. The screens are tough. You need to be ready.

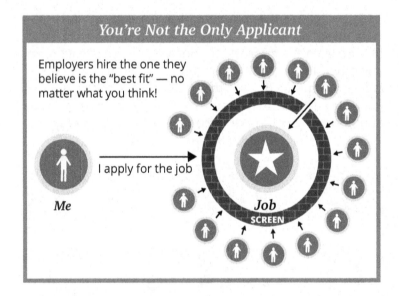

115

Process: There is a typical hiring process. Employers play a role. Candidates play a role.

There are myriad resources available addressing interview-ing skills and techniques, but there seems to be a gap re-garding a simple description of how the interview chain of

Typical Hiring Process Funnel

Employer Creates and Advertises Job Opening

Applications

Screening

Interview(s)

Offer

Job Filled

Job Seeker

JOB OPENING
- Network, Network, Network
- Know who you are, what you want, and what you bring to the party
- Prepare your tools: LinkedIn, resume, elevator pitch, interview skills, etc.

APPLICATIONS & SCREENING
- Apply as appropriate: online, in-person, any other
- Network to find additional 'ways in'
- Follow up (but don't be annoying)
- 'Answer' every 'ask': customized resume, cover letter, etc. using employer's words

INTERVIEW
- Be prepared, learn the language, know the job requirements, 'asks' and you
- Remember this is to screen people out
- Screener may/not know job deeply
- Interviews take many forms. Be prepared, confident, and professional
- 'Thank you' notes to all afterward

OFFER
- Thank employer for offer
- Short time to decide (some times 24–48 hours)
- May have some room to negotiate some items
- If you choose to negotiate, be realistic; remember, employer does not have to adjust
- Once accepted be clear on start date, then show up ready to learn and add value!

Employer

JOB OPENING
Defines:
- Business case for the job
- Requirements (deliverables; fit)
- Pay range (internal & external equity)
- Advertising methods to get top talent at best cost and speed

APPLICATIONS & SCREENING
- Receives and screens applications
- Focus on:
  » Screening 'OUT'
  » Finding top quality applicants to move forward
- Typically done by recruiters or HR

INTERVIEW
This phase is to:
- Vet the quality of applicants that appear to be best matches for opening
- May start with phone screen/interview
- Interview may involve a number of people, multiple appointments, and varying formats

OFFER
At this point, employers have made their choice and shift from screening you out to convincing you to accept and join them.

events unfold. Understanding the basics of each step and key actions for each will optimize your efforts and ultimately your career transition/job search results.

The above graphic attempts to close that gap by depicting the general flow of things (center) and several typical high-level actions and focus areas for job seekers (left) and employers (right).

There are innumerable variations to how talent acquisition work gets done. Some employers are much more rigorous, employing arduous, complex machinations. Others, not so much. Their recruiting process may be little more than a quick thought about some work that needs to get done, a few informal calls to get the word out, one or two informal chats, and an offer.

The person who receives an offer to fill an opening is the one the employer believes is best qualified and most likely to successfully *do the work they need done* and *fit with the culture*. If you haven't convinced the employer that you are the best possible candidate on both these counts, he/she will move on to someone else.

116

This process (especially early) is about screening people OUT.

★ Let's be clear — employers look for "best fit" as we define it.

★ We are inundated with applications and must screen down to a manageable few.

★ The process often starts with your application and/or resume being entered (either by you online or by the employer's team into an ATS [Applicant Tracking System]). These systems are looking for a simple word match. Fewer matches = less success.

★ It's critical that you use the employer's words; the computer doesn't know what you meant, and it doesn't look for synonyms.

★ If the ATS doesn't knock out your application/resume, the next step is for a person to review the job to look for BEST matches. Whether a recruiter, sourcer, human resources associate, or other, the people doing this screen may/not know anything about the job other than the job description they were given. Again, they are looking for easy matches, which makes it all the more important that you use the employer's words!

★ If your information makes it past this screen, it will now be reviewed by an HR leader and/or the hiring manager. These are more experienced eyes that are screening people out to get truly the "top few" they will interview.

117

Applying online is not generally effective. Most jobs are landed because of networking.

Application and screening — all the work you've done so far is leading to this — actually putting your name in the hat for an opportunity. Perhaps you read it online. Maybe someone told you of it. Maybe you heard about it some other way. The point is you found an interesting opportunity. Take a moment to celebrate. This means you have at least some idea of what you are looking for. Now is the time to get your name in front of employers.

Applying for jobs is about process and people. The process may require you to apply online, but don't expect that application to land you the job. To be successful, you need to connect with people.

★ Applying for a job online is one of the least effective ways to actually land a job. Often less than 5% of jobs are filled via online applications.

★ The vast majority of jobs are filled via networking and personal referrals — often upwards of 80%.

Key points regarding application and screening:

★ Always apply as directed in the job posting (online, in person, other).

★ In addition, NETWORK to find and connect with people who can open other ways in.

★ After you've applied, follow up if you don't hear anything (but don't be annoying); a good rule of thumb is 10 days to two weeks after applying.

★ Ensure all your documents (resume, cover letter, etc.) "Answer" every "Ask" and use the employer's language (not Mil-speak or Veteran-ese).

★ Applications are typically received and screened by recruiters (internal team members or contracted vendors) and/or HR staff. Their focus is on:

  ★ Screening OUT applications that do not meet their expectations for any reason.

  ★ Finding top quality candidates to move forward in the process.

STORY

A gentleman in career transition (let's call him Roger) sees an online posting for a project manager position that interests him. The company, the location, the de-

scription of the job all piqued his interest. The online advertisement required application online..."just click the link." He did so. A week went by. He heard nothing. Two weeks. Three. A month later he received a generic rejection email "thanks for applying; the position has been filled." As you might expect, Roger was disappointed. He went to the local pub that evening and ran into a buddy he hadn't seen in a few months. This buddy was celebrating. He just landed a new project manager job! As he relayed his success story, it was clear that he had been hired into the job Roger applied for. Roger was happy for his buddy but a bit torqued that he was overlooked; after all, he had much more experience. Roger kept his wits about him and asked his buddy how he did it. His buddy's reply? "I saw the opening online. I applied as directed, then I checked my network. I looked on LinkedIn, through my email contacts, etc. to see if I knew anyone at that company. Turns out I did! I reached out, told them what I was interested in and asked if they had any insights or connections that might help. One friend was able to give me her perspective on the business and the culture. Another actually knew the hiring manager. Another works in HR. I asked them if they'd be willing to get my resume in front of whomever might help. They did. Shortly thereafter I received a call for a phone interview and the rest is history!"

118

Some employers post phantom jobs just to see what the employment market looks like.

It's always good to understand your environment and its various dimensions. In the Army, we use "IPB" (Intelligence Preparation of the Battlefield). While employers don't use that term, all do some degree of intelligence gathering. It is quite prominent in sales, business development, and marketing functions.

Savvy HR leaders keep their thumb on the pulse of the employment market. They may read various reports, network with colleagues, and take other actions to be current on the state of talent availability and trends. Occasionally they post phantom jobs — jobs that really don't exist, but by posting and receiving responses, they get an idea of the volume and quality of talent that is in the market and interested in opportunities.

As an applicant, you likely won't know if this is the case for the specific opening that caught your eye. Apply and exploit opportunities that may arise from it. Meet and talk with relevant people. Network with others who might make you smarter and/or open more doors. If it goes somewhere, great! If not, consider it a "practice" round; one more evolution in your transition journey, and one more opportunity to improve your transition knowledge, skills, and abilities.

119

Resumes, cover letters, referrals, and interviewing — resumes are a ticket to the party.

Resumes are critical. They alone won't get you a job, but without a good one, customized to the opportunity, you likely won't get called for an interview.

Employers and their teams are busy, and your resume is likely one of many. Folks simply don't have time to review, assess, and consider it long. In fact, the first look is often 6 to 10 seconds. If the reader has any concerns whatsoever, you're out of the game right then.

So, what are employers looking for on that first screen?

★ Is it easy to read?

★ Are format and font simple and consistent?

★ Is the content clear, concise, and complete, focusing on results?

★ Are there unexplained time gaps?

★ Does it include *their* words? (or is it filled with Mil-speak/Veteran-ese they don't understand)?

Often resumes are screened by an ATS (Applicant Tracking System), which does a word-match comparing your resume to the job requirements. The more words that match, the better your chances of getting a real human being to give it a look.

A best practice is to build a base version and build job-specific versions for every job to which you apply. By doing so, you have all of your info on the base versions, and the custom versions highlight your "Answers" to each of the employer's "Asks" — using their language.

120

Cover letters, like resumes, are tickets to the party.

Not every employer asks for cover letters. If they don't ask, you may choose to provide one. If they do ask, you need to provide one. Cover letters are not resumes. The purpose is to show that you are both interested in the opportunity and interesting enough to cause the employer to call you in.

121

Referrals work! If someone I know/trust recommends you, I'm going to listen.

Referrals can be the secret sauce to getting your information in front of decision makers while everyone else's online applications swirl around.

Receiving a referral from someone in my network makes a huge difference.

I look at three "Rs."

* ★ Reputation.

* ★ Relationship.

* ★ Relevance.

If their reputation is positive, our relationship is established and their input is relevant to the open job in question, I'm going to listen. Your information WILL get a special look.

To be clear, a value-adding referral does not have to come from a small "inner circle" of colleagues. As long as the referral meets the Three R's above, you'll go to the top of the pile.

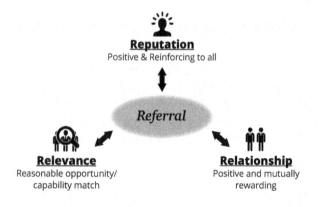

Reputation
Positive & Reinforcing to all

Referral

Relevance
Reasonable opportunity/
capability match

Relationship
Positive and mutually
rewarding

STORY

A stranger knocks at your door. How do you react? What do you do? Likely you are cautious. You may/not open the door. If you do, you may/not be guarded in your conversation.

Let's assume you open the door and chat. Then this stranger asks to borrow your car to make a trip to the local hardware store to pick up tools and materials to fix his leaky toilet. Do you loan this stranger your car? Not likely!

Now, let's change things up a bit. One of your best friends calls you and says his brother-in-law (who you've never met but have heard is a good guy) has an urgent house problem and needs to get to the hardware store. Their wives have taken their cars for the day, so neither of them has a car available. He asks if you will let him borrow yours. Being a good friend whose judgement you trust, you agree. When the brother-in-law knocks at your door, you open it and willingly toss him the car keys.

Referrals matter.

122
Next up — interviewing!

Assuming you make it through the application and screening process, you likely will be invited to interview.

General interview tips for candidates:

★ Be prepared, learn their language, know the job requirement "Asks" and be prepared to "Answer" everyone.

★ Remember, interviews (especially early) are designed to screen people out and discover the candidate that best matches the job needs.

★ Be aware that interviewers and others in the process may not know the job deeply.

★ Interviews may take many forms. Be prepared, confident, and professional even if the format is unexpected.

    ★ Phone screens/interviews are often the first step.

    ★ Interviews may involve a number of people and multiple appointments.

★ Send "Thank You" notes to everyone involved in the interview. (It really does make a difference since few people actually do it.)

123

Interviewing is not a natural act for most people.

Many folks in career transition/job search have very little experience interviewing.

Despite these truths, interviewing is a real thing. It remains a critical, unavoidable component of the hiring process. It is the part of the process where employers get to know you and vet you against their needs.

124

There are often several different players in the recruiting/interview/selection process (and many of them are not recruiting professionals).

Lots of people play in this world. Each of these have different perspectives, purposes, experience, expertise, and expectations. As with so many things, the employment process succeeds due to the good work of many different people. Every company is structured uniquely and uses different titles for their jobs. There is no absolute single way to get this work done. Below are some typical different titles and the duties they may generally perform.

* ★ *Hiring Manager:* The hiring manager is typically the person responsible for the job opening in the first place. This is the person who says, "This is what I need and when I need it." He/She is facing some set of circumstances that require an additional person to join the team. This may be because an incumbent left, maybe business is growing, or there was a restructure that requires a person with a set of experiences or skills that no current employee has.

* ★ *Human Resources (Associate, Partner, Leader, Manager, Director, VP, or any number of other titles):* This is the staff professional who supports hiring managers for all people-related topics, of which filling jobs is only a part. Their role is to enable successful operations, optimize engagement, and ensure policies, processes, and practices are in place that are compliant with all relevant laws, rules, regulations, and similar internal and external requirements.

* ★ *Talent Acquisition Team:* The company may or may not have a dedicated talent acquisition team (smaller companies often don't, in which case HR often covers these duties). Where these teams exist, they are charged with advertising the opening (making it known to intended markets using various methods and media), receiving and screening applications, conducting initial phone screen interviews, coordinating in-person interviews, and perhaps even drafting offer letters (based on close coordination with HR and the

hiring manager). There may be various titles for folks on this team (e.g., recruiter, talent acquisition specialist, sourcer, scheduler, workforce planner, etc.). Don't get too wrapped around the axle about titles — just use good common sense to understand who's playing as you engage an opportunity.

★ ***The company may also use external recruiters/search firms.*** These are vendors the company hires to find and present talent to them. External recruiters are either *retained* (paid a fee to fill a job) or *contingent* (only paid when the job is filled). For professional, salaried roles, most employers prefer to use retained search firms. I cover this here only as an FYI. Whether *retained* or *contingent*, it makes little difference to you — in either case you don't pay anything to the recruiter, the company does. Because of this it's important for you to remember — the recruiter does not work for you. The recruiter works for the company. This is not a slight on recruiters. I have many fantastic recruiter friends. But the facts are the facts. Recruiters work for those who pay them — the employer.

★ ***Approving Authority:*** This may be the hiring manager, it may be the next level manager, or someone even higher up. As a general rule, the tighter the business conditions, the higher the approval level is. Typically, the approving authority's role is to ensure that the money is right. They authorize the position and the spend to fill it.

   Note: Once the position is advertised, the Approving Authority may choose to cancel, delay, or change approval to fill it. Business conditions change and these folks have to adjust to them. This is another point where a great network and strong relationships matter. If you have them, you may hear about changes before others do and/or may be able to work out an alternate path around the changes.

★ ***The Interview Team:*** Interviews are rarely one-person events. Most often, several people interview select candidates. This may be just a couple of individuals or it may be several. (The most I've ever seen was 10.)

125

Never underestimate what you don't know.

As you progress through the recruiting and interviewing process be aware that the various players may have different motivations.

The vast majority will be honorable, well-intended folks with generally aligned expectations, focused on ensuring the best possible talent joins their team.

You may come across someone, however, with conflicting priorities and intent who has little interest in objectively considering you for the position at hand.

They may be advocating for another candidate (internal or external). They may not want the job filled at all due to budget constraints (and they have another higher priority job they need to fill). They may simply not like the fact that you are a veteran (or have veteran-related or other biases).

You'll likely never know for sure who has what motivations. Keep your eyes/ears open. Stay situationally aware. If you sense that someone has a motivation that is counter to your purpose, use all your skills and experience to assess the situation, define the best path forward, and create the best outcome possible.

126

Past, present, future, performance, potential, passion, and pragmatism — all collide during interview and selection.

In the *present* the employer is considering your *past* performance to determine your *potential* to *perform* well in a job they need to fill in the near future.

The process is more art than science. Many folks in the mix are not interviewing experts. Some know little about the job requirements beyond a job description that they were provided shortly before the start of the interview. Some have unstated expectations that have little to do with the documented job specs. Some have personal agendas.

Recognize it for what it is — an imperfect process, designed and conducted by humans with all the positive and negative potential of any human process.

Do your homework. Prepare diligently. Use all available resources to understand what the employer is Asking for and prepare your responses to Answer every Ask, using language the employer will understand.

Leading with your passion (your "why") may be powerful. Pairing it up with pragmatic, relevant evidence of your past performance, stated in a language the interviewer understands, might just create a win!

127

The interview begins the second you hit my property.

My security guards, reception staff, and others are paying attention. I check with them to see how you behave and interact. If you're a jerk, you may be gone.

128

We don't know how to interview you — make our job easy by speaking our language.

STORY

A CEO, a golfer, a cricket player, and a football player go to a bar...

The golfer proudly cites his winning game today, noting his low number of strokes.

The cricket player chats about his win describing runs and wickets.

The football player eagerly discussed his game-winning touchdown run.

The CEO sits quietly sipping some Pappy, relishing in his company's outstanding profitability and the resulting growth in share price.

All winners. All scoring differently.

None would hire the others if they couldn't describe their ability to score and win the game they're in.

Tell your story in a way that lands well on employers' ears.

129

There are several different interview styles.

Every organization interviews differently. That said, there are several common interview formats and approaches you might experience. Whether in-person or virtual, each will challenge you in a unique fashion. Don't be surprised if the interview cycle includes several different styles.

★ **Traditional interviews:** The traditional interview is a common interview format that you might expect with questions like, "Tell me about yourself," "What's your biggest strength?" and "What experience is most relevant to this job?"

★ **Behavioral interviews:** These interviews ask you to tell stories of your past experiences in a structured way. This structure has many variations but all generally focus on "SAR" — situation, action, and result. These interviews seek to determine if you can frame your experience and responses in a logical, detailed way that helps us understand the circumstance, the actions you took, and the results you created. These include questions like, "Tell me a time when you were under intense pressure." When asked "Tell me a time..." cite a specific example. Don't generalize. We'll see through it right away.

★ **Technical interviews:** These interviews explore your expertise in a particular field. For example, if interviewing as an engineer, you may be asked to solve a math problem. If being interviewed as a nurse, you may be asked to diagnose a hypothetical patient.

★ **Live test interviews:** In this interview format, you will be given a packet of materials and asked to analyze/use these materials and produce a certain output. For a financial analyst, you may be asked to calculate particular financial metrics from a given set of data. For a mechanic, you may be provided a disabled piece of equipment and asked to diagnose and repair it.

★ **Case interviews:** In this type of interview, you will have a scenario to solve. For example, "After being a market leader in the business' product space, we are now facing declining sales in three of five markets. Please describe how you approach defining the root cause(s) of this negative trend." This is an interactive interview style. You will be asking the interviewer questions and describing your approach, analysis, decision process, and other areas of interest for the employer.

★ **Stress interviews:** These interviews are used to see how you handle pressure and stress. If you respond negatively, you likely will not be the top candidate. While these are never fun interviews, it is far better to know how you respond to stress now than after you are hired.

★ **Presentation interviews:** Pretty straightforward; you will be asked to present material that you prepared ahead of time.

★ **Social interview:** These interviews transpire over drinks or a meal. The focus is on your professionalism and manners, and how well you fit in with peers, managers, clients, partners, and other stakeholders relevant to the job.

It's also important to know that while most interviews (regardless of style) are one-on-one, there are several other ways interviews may be conducted.

★ **Panel interviews** involve you interviewing with several people at the same time.

★ **Round-robin interviews** cycle you through several different people, moving to their location one after another.

★ **Rotation interviews** are similar to round-robins, but you remain in the same location and interviewers come in/out to interview you.

Employers may select these different styles based on myriad reasons, some of which may be nothing more complex than availability and efficiency. Don't let the style get you off track. They are looking for the best person to join their team. Prepare well and demonstrate that you are that person.

130

Do your interview homework.

The interview is the time for you to convince me and others that you are the best person to do the work I need done and fit/add value to my team.

If you didn't do the work to robustly prepare for the interview, how can I trust you'll do the real work on the job?

Know the job description. Have some understanding of the company, our products, our situation, our history, our leadership, our opportunities, our headwinds, etc.

Have some good questions ready for us (focused on how you can best help us — not how we can best help you).

Tips before the Interview

Know the job. Understand what the employer is asking for. Prepare your Answers for every Ask.

★ Research the company, industry, and the competition.

★ Prepare and practice your personal pitch.

★ List questions to ask the interviewer.

★ Be sure your references are cool being references.

★ Conduct mock interviews and practice, practice, practice.

★ If in person, figure out where you are going; if virtual, test your systems and connections and prepare your location and lighting well ahead of time.

★ Prepare materials to bring with you. (Copies of your resume on quality paper, references, pad and pen for notes, directions/connection instructions, company and interviewer contact info, interview instructions, etc.)

★ Immediately before arrival/when the interview starts, do a final "bio-break" and appearance check.

Upon arrival/interview start

★ Arrive/connect to virtual system early (15 minutes).

★ Be professional with ALL people you encounter (employers will ask what others thought of you).

★ Prepare a professional, positive greeting. You never get a second chance to make a first impression.

While Interviewing

★ Sit up straight. Smile. Maintain eye contact. Don't fidget.

★ Listen. Understand what you are being asked. Pause if you must, ask a clarifying question if you must, but pay attention. Skilled interviewers pay attention to whether you even understood the question they asked.

★ Be alert and agile. Listen to the tone the interviewer(s) set. It is an insight to their culture.

★ Be you. Engage with the interviewer(s) genuinely. Converse naturally — remember, you are interviewing them also!

★ Ask your questions as appropriate. Most often, this is near the end but some interviewers prefer a more conversational approach and invite you to ask questions along the way.

★ When the interview wraps up, thank the interviewer(s) for the opportunity. Reiterate your interest. Offer to answer any additional questions. Ask for contact info for all interviewers if you don't already have it.

After the Interview

★ Send Thank You emails and handwritten notes. Reiterate your interest.

★ Follow up later (call or email) at a reasonable time (usually about two weeks) to check on progress.

131

Yes, overqualified is a real thing. Sometimes problematic. Sometimes not.

The concept of proportionality, using the right weapons/tools/tactics for the situation, is well known in the military. B52 bombers aren't often used where small arms will suffice. As a normal course of business, Sergeants Major don't do E5 work.

Similar conventions exist in the civilian world. Being the best fit for a particular opportunity means your capabilities are generally aligned with the needs.

Employers' concerns about being overqualified are well founded. I've seen it countless times. Among the concerns are that such a candidate:

★ Will try to make the job bigger/other than it is.

★ Will get bored quickly and seek other opportunities.

Being overqualified is not, however, an automatic disqualifier for all opportunities. It may be a positive if the employer:

★ Is looking for someone to expand the job as the business grows.

★ Seeks to fill a talent pipeline for future, larger roles.

Learn all you can about the opportunity, the specific qualifications and deliverables, the company, and the hiring manager.

Present yourself as the best candidate to do the job and fit on the team.

Keep your eyes/ears open for insights that help you gauge whether your qualifications are too much, too little, or just right.

132

Most interviewers and employers can smell fear.

Employers seek confident, capable people to join their teams — partners, if you will. We understand that the interview and selection process can be nerve-wracking and expect a bit of nervousness at first. That said, if we get the sense that you are scared or fearful in the interview or about the opportunity, you're appeal will drop notably.

Be confident. Be bold. Be professional. Show us how and why you are the top person to fill our needs.

133

Cocky will kill you.

As mentioned in the "General" chapter *competence* and *confidence* are both critical to success; balancing them is the secret sauce.

When interviewing, it's important that you present both, but if you get cocky, you will come off as a non-team player who is out for yourself. Few employers find that appealing. Be honest about the value you truly bring. Focus on my needs. Drop the ego. Get over yourself, and show me how you are the best candidate. Remember — it's never good to "over-promise" and "under-deliver."

> ### *STORY*
>
> *I once interviewed a highly capable gentleman who had a great resume and top-notch references. He was clearly capable, with great technical potential. When I invited him into my office to start the interview I led with "Hi in-sert name why are we here today?" His reply? "I'm here for you to convince me why I should consider this opportunity." Shortest interview ever.*

134

Look me in the eyes. Smile.

Interviews are about interaction. Yes, I want to hear the content of your responses, questions, and comments, but

I'm also looking at how you interact with me, your body language, your general demeanor, etc.

Eye contact goes a long way in establishing and maintaining connection.

Smiling shows me you are friendly, composed, interesting, and interested.

135

I'm listening to hear if you understand and can answer the questions I'm asking.

Communication is a two-way street. Sending your message is one thing. Receiving others' messages is something else. When interviewing, one measure of how well you might fit our needs is if you can even understand the questions I'm asking. If I ask a question, it is OK to ask for clarification. If you have to ask for clarification for EVERY question, it may raise concerns. If, on the other hand, you blather an irrelevant answer to a question you don't understand or try to "pivot" the topic to something else, you are treading on thin ice.

Listen to the questions. Answer them clearly, concisely, and completely. It will leave a positive impression!

136

The killer interview question — "What is your greatest weakness?"

Interviewer — "What is your greatest weakness?"

Candidate — "I'm too honest."

Interviewer — "I don't think that's a weakness."

Candidate— "I don't care what you think."

This question is about self-awareness, introspection, self-development, transparency, and willingness and ability to discuss tough issues.

Suggestions for responding:

1. State your weakness clearly and concisely.

2. Move quickly to actions you've taken to improve.

3. Wrap up with a success story demonstrating improvement.

STORY

Worst interview question I've ever heard? "What color dry-erase pen is hardest to erase from the whiteboard?" It was asked by an inexperienced associate and was thoroughly irrelevant to the interview. For whatever reason, his expected answer was "blue." I responded, "The one that's been on the board longest." By his reaction you'd have thought I solved world peace.

137

Leverage is inherent in the recruiting process; employers have it early. You gain some near the end.

Experienced recruiters, HR leaders, and hiring managers understand leverage and how use it. Candidates who truly want to be successful need to recognize it and understand how to deal with it. A few things to consider:

★ Source of the leverage.

★ Its magnitude.

★ Impact on you (positive or negative).

★ Your ability to influence it.

★ Limitations it may cause and opportunities it may generate.

As you prepare for transition, consider mentorship from folks skilled in this area. Often these may be from sales, business development, procurement, law, and/or marketing-related fields. (Although folks from other functions may be highly skilled also.)

If you are seeking to fill an open job, the employer has the leverage. They own the opportunity, and they call the shots. You likely will have dozens or hundreds of competitors — most of which are every bit as qualified as you and some who are far more qualified than you. Be responsive; be proactive; be respectful of the employer's situation. Make their job as easy as possible. Remember that the early phases of this process are to screen people out. Don't give them an excuse to exclude you and move on to the other great candidates.

On the other hand, if the employer seeks you out, approaching you about an opening, the leverage balance shifts — you now have more leverage, in that they want you more than you want them. You can be a bit more selective, maybe even playing a bit hard to get. That said, remain professional, respectful, and appreciative — it will go a long way in reinforcing their desire to have you on their team.

Once the process gets to the offer stage, you gain a small amount of leverage. At this point, they have invested time and energy in you. They made a decision that you are the best fit to do their work. Losing a selected candidate at this point is a huge negative for recruiters. Be wise in your negotiations, continue to demonstrate that you are the best person to fill their need, and always remain professional!

138

"Answer" all my "Asks."

Early in your transition you likely won't have a specific job opening in mind.

That said, clarifying your target early, then shifting as needed while you progress through your transition journey helps to begin clarifying your understanding, refining your responses to potential interview questions, and better preparing yourself for success.

To do this, I recommend the "Ask — Answer" approach. Job postings, job descriptions, and advertisements generally include a listing of the duties, responsibilities, scope, deliverables, experience, education, and other requirements the employer seeks for that job. It tells readers what the employer is Asking for. All of your information, material, responses to conversations, and interview questions are your Answers. The employer takes all of it in and makes decisions based on how well you Answer all their Asks. They use this to decide if you are the best person to:

★ Do the work they need done.

★ Fit on their team.

Gather some information about the kind of job you seek. Do some research. Collect a number of job postings, descriptions, and advertisements. Combine the various information in the Asks column of a simple two-column sheet.

Next, for every Ask, begin to note your Answers in the right column. At first, don't worry about right/wrong; just record your answers. As you continue your transition work, your base of knowledge will grow. Your answers will get better. Your confidence and clarity will improve.

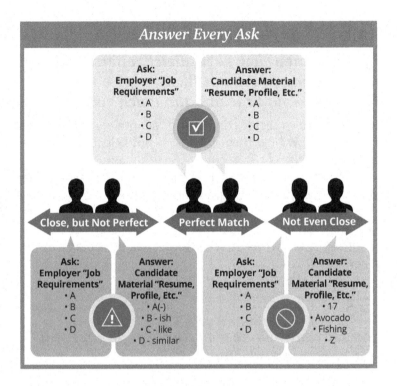

Why is this so important? As I mentioned earlier, this process, especially early on, is about screening people out. There are often many applicants for open jobs and good people are often working many openings simultaneously. The first look lasts only a few seconds. Your resume must make an immediate impression — or you are out of the game. During the interview process, you need to demonstrate that you are the candidate that matches all their needs. The best way to do this is to Answer every Ask using the employer's language!

139

After the interview — feedback, offers, and negotiations: We're not likely to give you feedback — no time and too much risk.

It's normal to expect feedback after an interview. Everyone wants to know how they did and, if not selected to move forward, why.

The unfortunate fact is that most employers won't give you such feedback. They are simply too busy and providing such feedback can open doors to potential negative events like discrimination complaints. You are welcome to ask for feedback but don't be shocked when you get no answer or a very generic reply.

140

You may have done everything right and still not have been selected.

Competition for most jobs is fierce. There are many quali-fied people in the mix and employers often have to make tough decisions between two or more highly capable peo-ple. Even if your interview(s) went great, you may not be se-lected. You'll never really know what happened or why they selected someone over you. This is more art than science and sometimes experience, intuition, and gut feel play into making these tough, tight decisions amongst qualified candidates.

If this happens to you, don't despair. Do a personal after-action review (AAR). Define what went well (so you can replicate it) and what you can do better, then move on. I can assure you — the employer already has. Remember, your future is ahead of you, not behind you.

141

If not selected, be professional.

Don't burn a bridge; we might just remember you. If you remain positive, we might have a different, better job for you now or later.

142

At some point, you will receive an offer.

After all your work, transition preparation, networking, re-sumes and LinkedIn profiles, interviewing, and so on, this is going to feel GREAT! It should! It represents a success in your journey.

143

Celebrate your success but remember an offer letter is a business document, not a love letter.

'Nuff said?

144

Key points to remember about the offer.

When employers make an offer, they have made their choice as to whom they believe is the best candidate to fill their open job. Their focus shifts. No longer are they look-ing to screen you out. They are now focused on convincing you to accept the offer and join the team.

As the selected candidate, be aware of the following and act accordingly:

★ Thank the employer for the offer.

★ You will likely have a short time (sometimes 24 to 48 hours) to decide if you'll accept.

★ You may have some room to negotiate some items. If you choose to negotiate, be realistic and remember, the employer does not have to adjust.

★ Once you accept the offer, be clear on the start date and then show up ready to learn and add value!

145

Offer letters are rarely random, thrown-together documents.

Most employers do notable diligence to ensure the offer letter is written to accurately reflect expectations, terms, and conditions relevant to the opportunity. The information typically might include:

★ Job title.

★ Boss' name and title.

★ Department/business unit.

★ Work location.

★ Compensation (wage/salary, incentive/bonus plan information, if any).

★ Benefits eligibility (details are usually covered in a separate document).

★ Healthcare.

★ 401K (or similar retirement/deferred compensation).

★ Relocation eligibility, vacation, etc.

★ Duties and responsibilities overview.

★ Start date (usually within 2 weeks).

★ Instructions for acceptance (usually sign and return within 24 to 72 hours).

★ Notice that the offer is contingent on passing various pre-employment screenings.

146

You may get a verbal offer before they send the written offer.

This is common. It is a clear sign of the employer's desire for you to join their team. Thank them for the call and express your strong interest in receiving the written offer and joining the team. Make yourself available for further questions and calls.

Once you receive the written offer, read it carefully, assess the content, and take note of any instructions for follow up. You don't want to miss a deadline or requirement.

147

Offer letters are often contingent (usually on passing background, drug and/or other tests).

"Once you receive a job offer, keep networking and searching until you cash the first paycheck." That's some of the most valuable and pragmatic career transition advice I've ever heard.

So, what is an offer?

★ It is a written document that specifies the terms and conditions of employment.

★ It is NOT a casual conversation about pay, benefits, start date, and various other bits.

Why are they contingent? Simply, to protect the company. Contingent offers basically say, "We want you to work here. We believe you are the best person to do the work we need done and to fit well and add value to our team. These are the 'terms and conditions of employment.' To ensure we are complying with all requirements and to protect our business and our people, we are going to do some background and other checks, to verify there is nothing in your history that is inconsistent with law," etc.

Don't be scared of a contingent offer. Checks usually only take a few days, and if you've nothing to hide, you've nothing to worry about.

148

We can rescind an offer for any reason or no reason.

Truth. It happens, but not often. When it does, we don't have to tell you why.

If it happens to you, be professional. Express your disappointment, reaffirm your interest in our company, and stay positive. We thought enough about you to make an offer. If you haven't done anything to change that positive impression, we may just have another opportunity for you in the future or be willing to recommend you to a colleague who might have a great opportunity. (Yes, we network too.)

149

Negotiating an offer is an art.

Depending on the company and the role, job offers may be more/less negotiable. Most often the employer's first offer is darn close to best and final. Remember, most employers seek to get the best talent available for the least cost possible.

That said, if there are terms about which you have serious concerns and that, after having done your homework, you believe are out of line, you are free to attempt to negotiate. If you choose to negotiate, do it all in one shot. Bring all your concerns in one package. Coming back for multiple bites at the apple will usually not be well received.

Some terms are more frequently open for negotiation. (Every employer is different, so there are no "absolutes" here).

★ **Base pay** — usually some room for minor variation.

★ **Incentive/variable pay** — rarely open for negotiation as it is heavily regulated compensation with specific parameters.

★ **Retirement contributions** — rarely open for negotiation as they are heavily regulated programs with specific parameters.

★ **Health benefits** — rarely open for negotiation, as they are heavily regulated programs with specific parameters.

★ **Other benefits** — vacation, flexible schedule, and various others may be more open to negotiation.

Note: Sometimes employers EXPECT you to negotiate, due to the nature of the job. For example, a buyer or purchasing manager had better know how to negotiate. Doing so in response to an offer may be a perfect opportunity to demonstrate your skills.

150

Know your value. Be realistic. Know that opinions will vary.

Think of a treasured family heirloom. It has great value to family members. They love this item, what it represents, the memories it evokes.

At some point, someone decides to get it appraised by a recognized expert in the relevant field. When the appraisal comes back far lower than anyone expected, they discover that "value" is a relative term.

Similarly, when you are considering a job offer, you need to know your value — in the context of the offer and from the perspective of the employer making the offer.

Most employers do sound diligence around compensation and benefits. They generally want to pay the least cost possible for the best talent, but they know that their offers must be competitive when compared to similar jobs, in similar industries, and in similar geographic areas.

Do your homework early. Research the pay ranges for the jobs, industries, and geographies you seek.

Understand that no matter how much you may *want* top-of-range or higher pay, the market is what it is. Unless you bring something exceptional to the table and have convinced the employer you are exceptional, you are not likely to get exceptional pay.

Think of an auction — different bidders for different items. When you have the item others want, the value goes up!

151

Offer accepted. Now what?

At some point, all your hard work will come to fruition. You will accept an offer for the job that meets your wants and needs.

Congratulations! This is a huge win and a turning point in your career transition journey.

Celebrate, and get ready for the next steps on your journey.

Just as your transition into the military was a huge change, your transition to your newfound civilian job/career will also mark a huge change. You will now be entering the world described in the preceding General and Culture chapters of this book.

The process by which this entry happens is often far less structured than you might expect. You will likely be "fed with a firehose," met with high expectations, and exposed to a barrage of unfamiliar people, processes, topics, taskings, and so much more. Oh, and by the way, you'll need to be producing results ASAP.

Fear not! You've done tougher things. You've learned much in your transition. You are ready, willing, and able to achieve success!

Be well my friends. Keep up the fire.

Made in USA - North Chelmsford, MA
1284820_9781737371403
02.24.2022 1640